When All Else Fails...
Read the Instructions

JAMES W. MOORE

When All Else Fails...
Read the Instructions

 Abingdon Press

12 13 14 – 25 24 23 22

This book is printed on acid-free recycled paper.

Library of Congress Cataloging-in-Publication Data

Moore, James W., 1938–
    When all else fails, read the instructions/James W. Moore. p. cm.
    ISBN 0-687-44918-9 (alk. paper)
    1. Beatitudes. 2. Ten commandments. 3. Love—Biblical teaching.
    I. Title.
BT382.M64 1993
241.5—dc20   92-24122

ISBN 13: 978-0-687-44918-7

In chapter 5, the *Chicago Tribune* story about Douglas from Bob Greene's column is used by permission of Voicings Publications, a division of Italicus Publications.
The excerpt from *Foundations of Reconstruction* by D. Elton Trueblood in chapter 9 is Copyright 1946 by Harper & Brothers. Reprinted by permission of HarperCollins Publishers.

Most Scripture quotations are from the New Revised Standard Version Bible, Copyright 1989 by the Division of Christian Education of the National Council of the Churches of Christ in the USA. Used by permission.
Some Scripture quotations are the author's own version.

For my family—
June, Jeff, Jodi, Danny
—and all the others who have
inspired me and taught me to love
the Scriptures

CONTENTS

CONTENTS

Introduction

John 1:1
In the beginning was the Word.

Some years ago when our children were young, our family made a shopping trip. At the front door of the store, there on display for all to see, was one of those backyard play-sets. It had everything—swings, rings, monkey bars, a slide, a ladder, a parallel bar, and a see-saw. It was love at first sight for our children. They were totally smitten with this magnificent, green and brown backyard play-set.

So to make a very long story short, we ordered one for our backyard. It arrived the next day in a huge box. Obviously, it was unassembled. You can't believe how "unassembled" it was! There was an unbelievable number of unassembled parts—large bars, small bars, brackets, braces, chains, bolts, and lugs and washers.

On the very top of this smorgasbord of parts was a booklet of instructions which I, in typical macho-style, tossed aside. Then I began the unenviable task of putting together the backyard play-set. I worked at it for hours, pulling out the various parts and attempting to assemble them, but to no avail. Try as I might, I could not make the gym-set look like the beautiful picture on the side of the box.

One futile attempt ended with not enough parts; another with parts left over. Finally I finished, thrilled that I had used every single part—only to discover that the slide wouldn't slide, the swings wouldn't swing, . . . and the see wouldn't saw! I was so aggravated and so exasperated. And my frustration was compounded by the incessant barrage of questions:

"Daddy, are you almost through?"

"Daddy, can we get on now?"

"Daddy, why is it taking so long?"

"Daddy, it didn't take Sally's father this long to put her play-set together."

About four hours into the project, I noticed a bright yellow card on the bottom of the box that had contained the play-set. There was some neat block printing on the yellow card. I picked it up and looked at it. It read:

"By the Way . . . When All Else Fails,
Read the Instructions!"

That's an interesting parable for us, isn't it? Life is like that. It's hard to put it all together when we fail to read the instructions. That's why the Bible is so important for us. It's our survival kit, our instruction manual. It has the answers we long for and the solutions we so desperately need to make life work.

Just think, if somehow we were able to bring together the brightest minds of all times, psychologists, professors, theologians, lawyers, judges, scientists, doctors, and historians, and ask them to write a basic handbook for living a sane, meaningful, and productive life; a handbook that would be both profound and practical, that would give straightforward instructions for zestful living. And then if we put all their thoughts together and refined them and edited them down to a series of basic principles for living, we would discover that such a handbook had already been written many years ago. What we would have would simply be an awkward and incomplete summary of "The Ten Commandments," "The Sermon on the Mount," and "The New Commandment of Jesus."

The point is: "It's in the Book!" We've had it all along! For nearly two thousand years, we have held in our hands the key to life—the instruction manual, the answer to the world's restless yearnings. Now, I am not suggesting that we can master the Bible in five minutes or in three easy lessons. I am not suggesting that finding life's answers in the Bible is as easy as thumbing through the answer pages in the back of a math book. No! Not at all. If we are to discover the great truths of the Scriptures, then we need to know how to study the Bible.

There is an old saying that proclaims: "I could get this mattress up the stairs if I could just figure out how to get hold of it!" This is true with the Bible. There are certain handles that enable us to get hold of it—or better put, cause it to get hold of us! Let me suggest four such "handles." At the risk of sounding simplistic, I want to sum up the Bible in four words. These four words, which all begin with the letter "C," serve as a helpful outline for the Bible and its amazing drama of redemption. Here they are: *Creation, Covenant, Christ, Church.* Let's take a look at these one at a time.

FIRST, THERE IS CREATION

The very first words of the Bible say it: "In the beginning, God created the heavens and the earth." God created the world intentionally, purposefully, orderly, systemati- cally. God created the world out of love and for love, and when it was finished, God looked at it and said, "This is good!" No Big-Boom theory here. No Cosmic-Accident theory here. To me, calling the creation of the world a cosmic accident is more ridiculous than saying that *Webster's Dictionary* is the result of a print-shop explosion.

The old argument still appeals to me, the argument in which we are asked to imagine a man crossing a field. The man sees a watch lying on the ground. The man has never seen a watch before and does not know what it is or what it is for. What will happen? He picks up the watch and examines it. He finds that it is composed of a metal case and a porcelain dial. He opens it. Inside he finds a complicated, but orderly arrangement of springs and cogged wheels and levers and jewels, all ticking away systematically. He looks at the hands on the dial, and he quickly sees that they are moving in a predetermined order.

Now, what does he make of this?

Does he say, "Well, I suppose that all these things—the metal, the springs, the wheels, the levers, the jewels, the porcelain—just by chance came together from the ends of the earth, by chance made themselves into all these various parts, by chance wound themselves up, by chance made themselves into a watch and set themselves going?" No.

If he has any powers of reasoning at all, he will be

12

bound to say, "I have found a watch. Somewhere there must be a watchmaker."

So, in like manner, when we find a universe that has an order more accurate than any watch, it is only natural to say, "I have found a world. Somewhere there must be a worldmaker." The Bible tells us in its first sentence (and on through the rest of its pages) that there is indeed a worldmaker . . . and it is none other than God. God is the Creator, the Ruler of all things, the Lord of all life. This is the first great theme of the Bible—*Creation*.

SECOND, THERE IS COVENANT

What is a covenant? It's a contract, a binding agreement, a pledge, a promise, a pact. The biblical covenant is the binding agreement God makes with us: *"I will be your God and you shall be my people."* To understand the covenant better, we need to put in two extra words. God says, "I will be your *only* God (no other Gods), and you shall be my *servant* people (not privileged people, not choice people, not holier-than-thou people, but servant people)."

In the covenant, God calls us to be servant people, ministers, missionaries, a light to the nations. As the Old Testament puts it, "We are blessed to be a blessing." "We are chosen not for privilege, but for service." In the Creation story, we see the dependable natural laws (like the law of gravity) introduced into the world, woven into the fabric of the universe.

Here in the covenant, we see the dependable spiritual laws also introduced into the world. We have learned from experience that life works best for us

13

when we honor and respect the natural laws of the universe. For example, I know that it would not be wise to jump off the church spire, or drop a brick on my foot, or step in front of a speeding car. If I did any of these, I would run head-on into the dependable laws of nature, and I would suffer the consequences of violating those laws.

In like manner, the Bible teaches us that there are dependable spiritual laws in this world, and that life works best for us when we honor and respect the spiritual laws of the universe. *The covenant reminds us that life works best for us when we put God first and reach out in service to others; that life works best for us when we love God and love people.*

God gave the covenant to Abraham: "I will be your only God and you shall be my servant people." But the people didn't get it. They kept backsliding. They continually broke the covenant. So God tried a second approach. God gave Moses the Ten Commandments to clarify and spell out the meaning of the covenant more specifically.

• The first four Commandments define the first phrase of the covenant: "I will be your only God":

No other gods before me.
No graven images.
No taking the Lord's name in vain.
Remember the sabbath day to keep it holy.

• And the last six Commandments show what it means to be God's servant people:

You respect your parents.
You respect the sacredness of life.

14

You respect the property of others.
You respect the vows of marriage.
You respect the truth.
You respect the good fortune of others.

But even with the Ten Commandments in hand, the people still didn't get it. They kept on breaking the covenant.

So next, God sent the prophets, who tried in all kinds of dramatic ways to call the people back to covenant faith.

The prophets used strong language: "Your hypocrisy is a stench in the nostrils of God. I hate your feasts. I despise your ceremonies. God wants love and truth and kindness and righteousness, not religious play-acting."

And then the prophets began to say, "It's gone too far. The people have drifted too far away from God. A Savior is needed for this hour. A Savior is needed to redeem the situation. A Savior is needed to bring us back to God." And that, of course, brings us to the third word.

THIRD, THERE IS CHRIST

Let me mention two verses of Scripture that encapsule the impact of Christ on this world.

• The first verse is in the prologue to John's Gospel: "The Word became flesh and lived among us . . . full of grace and truth" (John 1:14).

This means that Jesus Christ was the covenant wrapped up in a person, the covenant lived out before us. It's as if God said, "They are not getting it. They

15

don't understand my language—so I will show them! I will act it out before their very eyes. I will send my only Son into the world to show them the meaning of the covenant. He will show them the truth. He will show them my will." And when they asked Christ about the greatest Commandment, what did he say? "Love God with all your heart, soul, and mind's strength, and love your neighbor as you love yourself," or in other words, "I will be your only God, and you shall be my servant people."

• The other verse that sums up the work of Christ in the world comes from the apostle Paul. Writing to the church at Corinth, Paul said this:*"In Christ God was reconciling the world to himself"* (II Cor. 5:19).

On a lengthy airplane trip when I was reading a newspaper, I noticed those personal ads in the back of the classified section. A lot of people with initials are telling unnamed persons that they are forgiven. "You can come home," they say. Evidently they know who they are. "You can come home now, you are forgiven."

It occurred to me that that's what the cross means, and it reminded me of that story about the police officer who found a little boy sitting on the curb in the downtown section of a big city. The little boy was crying because he was lost.

The officer said, "Don't worry. I'll help you! Glance around and see if you can see anything that looks familiar." The little boy looked around for a few moments, and then suddenly his face brightened, because off in the distance he could see a church. It had a tall steeple with a cross on top.

The little boy said, "There! Look! If you can get me to

16

the cross, we can find the way home!" That says it all, doesn't it?

In Christ, God was reconciling the world to himself. God was on the cross, reconciling the world to himself. On the cross, God was bringing us home!

First, there is Creation. Second, there is covenant. Third, there is Christ.

AND FOURTH, THERE IS CHURCH

The task of the church is to continue the preaching, teaching, healing, caring ministry of Jesus Christ. That's the way we evaluate ourselves as a church. How well are we continuing his ministry of love? Jesus went to the cross. He came out of the tomb. He passed the torch to us, and then he ascended into heaven. However, he didn't leave us alone. He sent the Holy Spirit to empower us and to work through us. The hymn writer put it like this:

> God is my strong salvation:
> What foe have I to fear?
> In darkness and temptation,
> My light, my help, is near.
> Though hosts emcamp around me,
> Firm in the fight I stand;
> What terror can confound me,
> With God at my right hand?

When all else fails, read the instructions and remember those four great recurring themes in the Scriptures—Creation, Covenant, Christ, and Church.

Obviously, we can't cover all the instructions of the Bible in the pages that follow, but we can take a closer

17

look at three sections of Scripture that powerfully and dramatically underscore the key ethical lessons of the Bible:

- The Beatitudes
- The Ten Commandments
- The New Commandment of Jesus.

There is amazing help here for the living of these days. These ancient, time-honored instructions, though thousands of years old, are as fresh as the morning sun—and are as relevant today as they were when they were first spoken.

I

Instructions for Meaningful Living

The Beatitudes

When Jesus saw the crowds, he went up the mountain; and after he sat down, his disciples came to him. Then he began to speak, and taught them, saying:

1. Blessed are the poor in spirit, for theirs is the kingdom of heaven.
2. Blessed are those who mourn, for they will be comforted.
3. Blessed are the meek, for they will inherit the earth.
4. Blessed are those who hunger and thirst for righteousness, for they will be filled.
5. Blessed are the merciful, for they will receive mercy.
6. Blessed are the pure in heart, for they will see God.
7. Blessed are the peacemakers, for they will be called children of God.
8. Blessed are those who are persecuted for righteousness' sake, for theirs is the kingdom of heaven. Blessed are you when people revile you and persecute you and utter all kinds of evil against you falsely on my account. Rejoice and be glad, for your reward is great in heaven, for in the same way they persecuted the prophets who were before you.

Matthew 5:1-12

1
It's Hard to Be Humble

Matthew 5:3
Blessed are the poor in spirit, for theirs is the kingdom of heaven.

There is an old story about a football team that lost a game 78 to 0. The next day at practice, the coach was not happy. He pointed out to the players (as only a football coach can) that they did not play well. They did not execute the fundamentals of the game well at all. The fact was, they didn't do anything right. They didn't block properly. They didn't tackle correctly. Their running game was pitiful. Their passing was even worse. Their kicking was embarrassing.

So the coach said to them, "We have to get back to the basics."

Then he reached over, picked up a football, held it up in the air for all to see, and said, "Now fellas, this is a football!"

That's really getting back to the basics, isn't it? And that is precisely what Jesus is doing in the Sermon on the Mount as he gives the Beatitudes. The church people of his time (like those football players who lost 78 to 0) were not executing well. They had drifted away from the fundamentals of faith. Many of them were religious, but their religion was not impacting their daily living as it should.

So here in the Beatitudes, Jesus calls them (and us) back to the basics. Here he underscores the basic Christian attitudes that we should embrace and cultivate in our lives—and pass on to our children. In other words, Jesus is saying to us that the basic attitudes listed in the Beatitudes are significant and crucial and blessed because they represent life as God meant us to live it. That is, those who are humble-minded and merciful, those who are obedient and righteous, those who are genuine and courageous, those who work through grief and for peace—those are the ones who are living out the will of God. If you ever wonder about that, consider the alternatives: arrogance, vengeance, selfishness, hypocrisy. Certainly, those are not the will of God for us. As always, Jesus is right on target.

The first key in unlocking the great truths of the Beatitudes is to come to a better understanding of the first word that introduces each of them. The word *blessed*. What does it mean?

The Greek word *makarios*, translated here as *blessed*, is an interesting word packed with meaning, but difficult to translate into English. It really means more than "blessed." Some scholars have suggested that it could be better translated as "O how exceedingly happy," or "O how fulfilled," or "O how blissful," or "O how at one with God."

All these translations are helpful, but let me suggest another that I think we might be better able to understand and relate to. The word *blessed* here really means, "close to God" or "near to the heart of God." In other words: "close to God are the merciful"; "close to

God are the peacemakers"; "close to God are those who hunger and thirst for righteousness"; "near to the heart of God are those who mourn"; "O how close to God are those who are persecuted for righteousness' sake."

With that in mind, let's take a look at this first Beatitude. Here's how it reads: "Blessed (or close to God) are the poor in spirit for theirs is the kingdom of heaven." In many ways, this is one of the most difficult of the Beatitudes to understand, because to us, that phrase "poor in spirit" sounds so unattractive, so unappealing, so weak and docile and mamby-pamby. I mean, who wants to be "poor in spirit"? Who wants to be around people who are "poor in spirit"? We like people who are peppy and spirited and zestful and enthusiastic and full of life. "Poor in spirit" sounds so frail and feeble and unbecoming.

But that's not what Jesus means here—not "poor-spirited," or "lifeless"—not that at all. Well, what then does he mean by this strange-sounding phrase? It helps to remember that in ancient Hebrew, this phrase "poor in spirit" was used to describe the humble people. It was a glowing compliment reserved for those humble-minded people who put their whole trust in God!

That's what it meant then, and that's what it means for you and me now. That understanding makes this Beatitude so much more attractive. *The "poor in spirit" are the humble-minded, those who trust God completely.* This attitude is the opposite of arrogance and self-righteousness. God calls us to be humble, not haughty!

So, this first Beatitude could be expressed like this: "O how close to God are those humble-minded people who put their whole trust in God and who honor and serve God as the King of their lives." Now, let's break

23

this down a bit and be more specific. Let me underscore what I consider to be some very special qualities of these humble-minded people. I'm sure you will think of others.

HUMBLE-MINDED PEOPLE
TRUST GOD COMPLETELY

A major television network once aired a special "made-for-TV" movie titled "The Betty Ford Story." The movie was produced with the help, the support, and the encouragement of Mrs. Ford, to reveal, out of her own personal experience, the dangers of drugs and alcohol. Betty Ford was overwhelmed by the demands and stresses of being the first lady and by the debilitating pain of arthritis. Consequently, over time, she became addicted to medication and alcohol.

In the most powerful scene in that movie, her family confronts Mrs. Ford, and one by one, the children express their love and their concern for her. And then straightforwardly, they tell her what they are seeing—that she has become a prescription-medicine addict and an alcoholic. At first, she denies that she has a problem, but eventually she realizes what is happening and gets help.

In that poignant intervention scene, one of the children says this to her, "Mother, always before, when you had a problem, you turned to God and to your family, but lately you have shut us out. You have turned to medicine and drinking, and you are killing yourself." Betty Ford's daughter was saying something we all need to hear: You don't need a crutch; you have a Christ. You don't need a scapegoat; you have a Savior. You don't need drugs and drinks to hold you up and get you through; you have God! The humble-minded are those who realize that and put their trust in God.

Some years ago, the noted missionary John Paton went to live in a remote corner of Africa. He taught the native villagers the Christian faith. He introduced them to Christ. He baptized them and started a church there. Then he set about the arduous task of translating the Bible into their language so they could read and study the Scriptures. All went well until John Paton realized that they had no word in their language for the word *believe*. He was stuck. After all, you can't put a Bible together without the word *believe*, can you?

One day as he was grappling with this problem in his hut, one of the villagers came in for a visit. The native villager was exhausted from a hard day's work. He sat down and leaned back and then in his native language, he said how wonderful it is when you are tired to "lean your whole weight on something." Suddenly, a light bulb flashed in John Paton's mind. He had his answer. That's how he could translate the word *believe*.

To believe is to "lean your whole weight on God"—to do the best you can, the best you know, and then lean on God. The humble-minded are those who know how to trust God completely, how to lean their whole weight on God. Listen! If you have a problem, don't turn to drugs or drinks. Bring it to the church. Bring it to the altar. Bring it to God. The humble-minded people are those who trust God completely.

HUMBLE-MINDED PEOPLE
TREAT OTHERS RESPECTFULLY

Again and again, Jesus reminds us that when we seek life selfishly and arrogantly, we lose it; when we

25

humbly give it away, we find it. The surest way I know of to make yourself miserable is to be totally selfish, completely wrapped up in yourself with no thought of others, with no interest in anything else. Think only of yourself, what you want, what you like and how people ought to treat you—you will be miserable.

In *The Greatest Thing in the World,* Henry Drummond said, "Half the world is on the wrong scent in the pursuit of happiness. They think it consists in having and getting and in being served by others (when actually the reverse is true); real happiness consists in sharing and in giving and in serving others." The humble-minded know that—and they commit their lives to that.

Some years ago a man went to his pastor with a surprising request. He wanted the pastor to help him carry out his doctor's advice. His recent trip to the doctor had been prompted by some familiar complaints—recurring headaches, chronic indigestion, irritability, vague fears, nervousness, worry.

The physician knew the man pretty well, so he sat him down and talked to him like a "Dutch uncle": "These pills will bring temporary relief, but the only chance for a real cure is up to you. If you can learn to forgive instead of holding on to your grudges; if you can learn to care about persons instead of nursing your prejudices—in other words, if you can learn to love, you can get well. If not, I am afraid the future is pretty dark for you."

The man, jolted by the doctor's counsel, had come to his pastor, saying, "Teach me how to love, teach me how to reach out to others, teach me how to care."

The humble-minded are happy, exceedingly happy;

26

they are close to God because they have respect for others. They trust God completely, and they treat others respectfully.

HUMBLE-MINDED PEOPLE APPRECIATE EACH DAY

Humble-minded people realize that life is a gift from God, and they embrace life and celebrate life one day at a time, with gratitude and thanksgiving.

In our home, we have lots of plaques on the walls that people have given us across the years. Most of them have an inspirational or spiritual message. Some are painted, some are printed. Some are done in needlepoint. One says: "When you can't sleep, don't count sheep. Talk to the shepherd." Another says: "Make new friends, Keep the old; Some are silver, Others are gold." Still another says: "There is no difficulty that enough love cannot conquer." All of those are nice, aren't they? One of my favorites is the one that hangs in our kitchen: "What we are is God's gift to us; What we become is our gift to God."

Some people go arrogantly through life, demanding this, that or the other—presumptuous, brash, haughty, selfish, egotistical. But Christian people imitate the gracious, grateful, humble spirit of our Lord—living in day-tight compartments, thankful for each day we have, ever appreciative of God and God's generous blessings.

O how close to God are the humble-minded! They trust God completely. They treat others respectfully. And they live each day appreciatively.

27

2
Near to the Heart of God

Matthew 5:4
*Blessed are the those who mourn,
for they will be comforted.*

• I once received a poignant letter from a young minister who gave me permission to share some of his words:

> The most devastating event of my life occurred in April of 1989. My mother had had a pain in her side for a couple of weeks. Nothing could be found. Then the doctors took a cat-scan and discovered that her entire colon and liver were covered with cancer. In August of 1989, my mother died with her entire family gathered around the bed as she breathed her last.
>
> My mother was a beautiful person because of her deep faith in God and her commitment to her family. She never complained about her pain or about her life being cut short at the age of forty-nine. All through her suffering, she would say, "I thank God for my family and my life." The morning after my mother was diagnosed with terminal cancer [and until the day of her death] each morning my father would say, boldly, "This is the day which the Lord has made!" And courageously, my mother would respond, "Let us rejoice and be glad in it!" What faith!
>
> I have said all this . . . to let you know that I have been through a great deal and have struggled with this pain.

29

Through it all, my father has been a tremendous example and encourager for me. However, I have to tell you, grief hurts!

• A young couple came in to see me several months after they experienced one of life's toughest blows—the loss of a baby. With courage and faith, they were trying to put their lives back together. We talked about the traumatic experience they were going through and how difficult it was. Then suddenly, they asked me that hard, agonizing, heartbreaking question—"Jim, how long will we hurt?"

• The young man sitting across from me was in anguish. He was so penitent, so sorry, so ashamed of what he had done and the pain he had caused. He had finally come to his senses. For years and years, he had put his parents through a living hell. He had been angry, hostile, arrogant, rebellious. He had been thoughtless and cruel to them. He had used them, tricked them, lied to them, and embarrassed them. He had exploited their goodness as he pursued his selfish life-style in the "far country" of drugs and alcohol, amid one sordid mess after another. But then when he hit bottom, he cried out for help, and God was there! And now God is turning his life around, but still he lives with the haunting memories of the way he had treated other people and what he put his parents through.

He said, "I don't know how I could have been so selfish. I was so immature, so stupid—and now I hurt so deeply when I think of the pain I caused my family."

• On the other end of the telephone line was a good friend, a solid citizen, and a committed Christian. There was a grave concern in his voice.

30

"We need your prayers," he said. "Our grandson is headed for the war, and we are worried sick. He is so fine, so capable, and so young. It was so hard to see him go. We hope and pray for a peaceful settlement and for his safe return home."

He went on, "Why, O why, can't the nations of the world get along? Why can't we get along?" Then he added, "It breaks my heart! It must break God's heart, too!"

What is the common thread that runs through all these true-life vignettes? A young minister who has lost his mother; a young couple who had lost their beautiful baby; a young man in spiritual anguish, penitent over his sinful past; a grandfather worried sick about his grandson, and about his world, caught up in yet another tense, volatile, dangerous international conflict.

Well, the common thread is that all these people are hurting. They are all in pain because they are all in grief—and grief hurts! Sorrow, sadness, mourning, grief—whatever you want to call it, it hurts! By definition, *grief* is the pain we feel when we lose something that once was special to us. We all know the experience and the hurt that comes with it, and that's why this second Beatitude is so important. This is how Jesus put it: "Blessed are those who mourn, for they will be comforted."

Now, what in the world does that mean? What is the message of this second Beatitude for you and me? Well, to understand this Beatitude better, we need to examine its key words. There are three—*Blessed, Mourn,* and *Comforted.* In these three words, we find the keys that unlock the truth of this Beatitude, and also

God's greatest promise—to always be with us, especially when we are hurting. Let's look at these together.

THE FIRST KEY WORD IS *BLESSED*

As we have seen, the word *blessed* can be translated as "O how happy!"; "O how fulfilled!"; "O how extremely blissful!" But those translations seem to miss the mark in this second Beatitude, don't they? "O how happy are those who mourn" sounds like a contradiction. I think that here the word *blessed* means "O how close to God." "O how near to the heart of God are those who mourn!"

That's what this is all about. I have seen the truth of it so many times. Again and again, I have heard people in great personal sorrow say, "This is terrible. It's the worst thing that's ever happened to us. But we are going to make it because God is with us as never before." I think the reason we find God so powerfully present at a time of sorrow is because God is like a loving parent who wants to be especially close to the children when they are hurting.

A few years ago, a three-year-old girl in our church family became very ill. She's fine now, but she was so critically ill then that she had to stay in the hospital for many months. In all that time, her mother never once left her side. Her mother stayed right with her day and night, displaying an amazing strength that inspired all of us who know her. Her strength was made all the more fascinating because that woman is very small, petite, delicate, weighing little more than ninety pounds.

After it was all over and the daughter was fully

32

recovered, I asked that young mother, "How did you do it? How did you have the strength to do that?"

She looked at me, smiled warmly, and said, "She's my child. I love her more than breathing. She needed me. She needed me as never before. I had to do it. I had to be there for her!"

Being a parent myself, I understood. Being a Christian, I thought to myself, God is like that—a loving parent who wants to be especially close to his children when they are hurting. In this second Beatitude, the word *blessed* means "O how close to God!" "O how near to the heart of God are those who are hurting!"

THE SECOND KEY WORD IS *MOURN*

Actually, the word *mourn* means "to care deeply." The opposite is to be untouched, unmoved, unfeeling. It's very important to remember that grief is a by-product of love. And though it sounds like a cliché, it is still profoundly true that it's better to have loved and lost than never to have loved at all. In the Gospels, we read that Jesus wept. He had heard about the death of his friend Lazarus, and he saw how sorrowful and brokenhearted were the family and friends of Lazarus, and he cried with them.

When the people saw him crying, they said, "See how he loved him."

I have a pastor friend who has been teased for years about something he did the first time he led a communion service. Reading the ritual printed in the bulletin, he came to the sentence "Hear now from the Scriptures these comfortable words." Then there was left a blank space, so that the pastor could quote some favorite verse of Scripture as words of comfort. My friend went absolutely blank! And after a few moments of awkward silence, he blurted out the only verse of Scripture he could think of at the moment: "Jesus wept!"

But if you stop and think about it, those are comforting words, because they do indeed remind us of how deeply Jesus loves. To mourn is to care deeply. Jesus was a man of sorrows acquainted with grief because he loved deeply, he cared deeply.

In the Bible, the word *mourn* is used in three distinctly different ways. As we have seen, it is used to describe the grief experience—sorrow over some loss. That is the most obvious and common usage.

Second, *mourn* also is used to describe the experience of penitence, sorrow over our sins. All through the Scriptures, we see people falling down, tearing their clothing, crying out to God in their shame and sorrow. In the early days of the church, there was what was called the Mourners' Bench. To it would come those who were at the end of their rope; they had to have God. God was their only hope. In penitence they came, in mourning they came, in shame and sorrow for their sins they came, seeking God and forgiveness.

Third, the Scriptures use *mourn* to describe those who looked with sorrow on the troubles, conflicts, injustices, and hurts of the world. As someone once expressed it in a prayer: "O God, forgive us for looking at the world with dry eyes."

The word *blessed* here means "O how close to God," and the word *mourn* describes "those who care deeply." "Blessed are those who mourn, for they will

34

be comforted," or "O how near to the heart of God are those who care so deeply that sometimes it hurts, for they will be comforted."

THE FINAL KEY WORD IS *COMFORTED*

It is helpful to remember that the word *comfort* comes originally from two Latin words—*cum* which means "with," and *fortis*, which means "strength." When you put them together, of course, you have "with strength." The word *comfort* means literally "with strength." So this Beatitude carries with it a great promise: "To those who go through trouble and sorrow, God will give great strength!"

"Blessed are those who mourn, for they shall be with strength." You know, it's absolutely true. Those who go through the valley of mourning and come to the other side do indeed come out with a new strength—a new strength of character, a new and deeper understanding of life, a new ability to empathize with others, a new power to help others in trouble, a new sense of closeness to God.

Alexander Solzhenitsyn tells of a moment when he was on the verge of giving up all hope as a prisoner in a Soviet prison camp. He was working twelve hours a day at hard labor. He was existing on a starvation diet. And he had become gravely ill. The doctors were predicting his death. One afternoon while shoveling sand under a blazing sun, he simply stopped working, even though he knew the guards would beat him severely, perhaps to death. But he felt he just couldn't go on.

But then he saw another prisoner, a fellow Christian, moving toward him cautiously. With his cane the man quickly drew a cross in the sand, and then quickly erased it. In that brief moment, Solzhenitsyn felt all of the hope of the gospel flood through his soul. It gave him strength and courage to endure that difficult day and the hard months of imprisonment that followed. Alexander Solzhenitsyn was saved that day by the sign of the cross. That quick reminder of God's love and power gave him the strength to hold on. The poet put it like this:

> Hold on to God's hand with all your might,
>   and he will hold onto you;
> Trust him strong with childlike faith,
>   and his grace will see you through.

And Jesus put it like this: "Blessed are those who mourn, for they will be comforted."

3
Here Am I, Lord, Use Me!

Matthew 5:5
Blessed are the meek,
for they will inherit the earth.

In the late 1600s, the magnificent St. Paul's Cathedral was built in London. Upon its completion, the architect, Sir Christopher Wren, arranged for the royal family to have a private tour.

When they finished the tour, the king said to the architect, "This cathedral is amusing, awful, and artificial," and Sir Christopher Wren was absolutely delighted!

When the king described St. Paul's Cathedral as amusing, awful, and artificial, the architect was thrilled beyond belief! Do you know why? Because back then, the word *amusing* meant "amazing," the word *awful* meant "awesome," and the word *artificial* meant "artistic"! The king was paying Sir Christopher Wren the highest compliment!

The point is clear: Over time and across cultures and languages, words change their meanings. A classic example of that truth is found in the third Beatitude: "Blessed are the meek, for they will inherit the earth."

Of all the Beatitudes, this is the hardest to take, the most difficult to swallow. The difficulty here, of course, is with the word *meek*. I mean, who wants to be meek today? It sounds so weak and wimpy, so syrupy.

I once heard about a little boy who became frustrated with his mother one day because she kept referring to him as her "little lamb."

Finally the four-year-old couldn't take it anymore and he said, "Mama, I don't want to be your little lamb. I want to be your little *tiger!*"

That's the way it is with most of us. We would be ashamed of being called "meek" in the way we understand that word today. Meek people and meek nations are those with no guts, no strength, no backbone. Some "blessedness" may await them in heaven, we think, but here on earth they are pushed around and kicked in the teeth. Today, meekness is a synonym for weakness.

But when Jesus spoke this third Beatitude, that's not what he had in mind at all. For Jesus, *meekness* meant "obedience to God." Throughout the Bible, the word *meek* is used to describe those people who have committed themselves totally to doing the will of God and to being God's servants—those who have yielded themselves completely to God—like putty in God's hands.

It's helpful to remember that in the Old Testament, Moses (of all people) was called "the meekest" of men. Now, think about that. It was Moses to whom God appeared in the burning bush. It was Moses whom God called upon to lead Israel out of slavery. It was Moses who courageously laid his life on the line by standing before Pharaoh and saying, "Let my people go!" It was

Moses who received the Ten Commandments. It was Moses who brought the people out of Egypt through the Red Sea. It was Moses who led the people through the wilderness, through battle, and through discouragement, toward the Promised Land.

No question about it—Moses was one of the strongest leaders and most courageous characters in the whole Bible. Yet when we come to the twelfth chapter of the book of Numbers in the King James Version of the Bible, we find these revealing words: "Now the man Moses was very meek, above all the men which were upon the face of the earth." Moses was a man of meekness because he realized how much he needed God, and he gave himself completely to God. He obeyed God. He trusted God. He served God. He did God's will—and that's what it means to be meek. It's the opposite of arrogance, haughtiness, pride, and selfishness. The meek are those who humbly yield themselves to God, to be used as God's tools any way and anywhere God should choose. There is great strength in that.

Max Lucado, in *Applause of Heaven,* reminds us that if God can use ordinary inanimate objects (just everyday things) then God can use us. Lucado recalls how God used the staff of Moses to lead the people of Israel to freedom, the hurled stones of little David to turn back a giant, the saliva of Jesus to heal a blind man. He points out that when we freely offer to God what we have, whatever it may be, through the miracle of God's grace the mundane can be made majestic, the dull divine, the humdrum holy. He reminds us that when it comes to serving God, the key is not the *ability,* but the *availability.* And then Lucado writes:

39

Blessed are the meek. . . . Deliriously joyful are the ones who believe that if God has used sticks, rocks, and spit to do his will, then He can use us.

We would do well to learn a lesson from the rod, the rock, and the saliva. They didn't complain. They didn't question God's wisdom. They didn't suggest an alternative plan. Perhaps the reason [God] has used so many inanimate objects for his mission is that they don't tell him how to do his job!

It's like the story of the barber who became an artist. When asked why he changed professions, he replied, "A canvas doesn't tell me how to make it beautiful."

Neither do the meek.

The meek humbly offer themselves in obedience to God. Here am I, Lord, send me! Here am I, Lord, use me!

So in the Scriptures, *meekness* doesn't mean weakness or wimpiness or cowardice. To the contrary, it refers to the strength that comes from commitment to God, the poise that comes from trust in God, the gentleness that comes from imitating God's gracious and self-giving spirit, and the humility that comes from realizing how much we need God.

Blessed are the meek, those who yield themselves to God and become like putty in God's hands. To put it in outline form, the meek are those who are surrendered to God's will, are steadied by God's presence, and are self-giving for God's sake.

THE MEEK ARE
SURRENDERED TO GOD'S WILL

The daily prayer of the meek: "O Lord, Thy Will Be Done." Over the years, hymn writers have cherished this concept:

40

Have thine own way, Lord!
Have thine own way!
Thou art the potter, I am the clay.
Mold me and make me after thy will,
While I am waiting, yielded and still.

. . .

Take my life, and let it be
consecrated, Lord, to thee.

. . .

Melt me, mold me, fill me, use me.
Spirit of the living God, fall afresh on me.

If you ever wonder what it means to be meek in the biblical sense, then just remember the words of those songs. Remember also that the Greek word for *meek* is *praos*, which suggests the taming and training of wild animals. The meek are those who have been tamed and trained by God, to be used in God's service.

I once read an article about the training of Arabian stallions. Day after day, hour after hour, the stallions are taught to obey the master, to trust him completely, and to always respond promptly to his call. The master has a whistle, and when he sounds the whistle, the stallions are trained to stop, no matter what the circumstances, and come immediately to the master. Then as a final test, the stallions are placed in a corral in the desert, midway up a hillside. At the bottom of the hill is a beautiful oasis with crystal blue waters. The stallions stay in the corral for several hours under the blazing desert sun, until they are frantic for water.

Then the master stands at the top of the hill, and the stallions are released from the corral. Of course, they all head straight for the water. But just before they reach the water, the master blows the whistle. The horses who ignore the master's call and go on toward the water are considered not ready and must have further training. But the stallions who turn, despite their terrible thirst, and come immediately to the master are considered well-trained and they graduate. They trust the master completely. They put his will before their own.

Now, let me ask you something: Are you that obedient to God? That's what it means to be meek. It means to be totally surrendered to God's will.

THE MEEK ARE STEADIED BY GOD'S PRESENCE

Sometimes we get it all mixed up, don't we? We think that security, strength, and serenity lie in power, position, and possessions. That's what our world teaches us, doesn't it? But actually, that's not really true. In fact, trust in those things leads to fear and paranoia.

When Joseph Stalin was at the height of his power as the Soviet premier, he was literally afraid to go to bed. He had seven different bedrooms, and each could be locked tightly. He slept in a different one each night in order to foil any would-be assassins. He had five different chauffeur-driven limousines, each with curtains closed so that no one could tell which he was in. So deep-seated were his fears that he employed one servant whose only job was to monitor and protect his teabags.

The message is obvious. Happiness does not come from outer security. Happiness comes from inner stability, the inner strength that comes only from God's presence in our lives.

Some years ago, an older woman was called to testify in a dramatic trial. The opposing lawyer was known for being tough, even heartless, and he was really badgering her on the witness stand. Shouting loudly, pointing his finger, the lawyer was using all kinds of emotional tricks to upset and fluster the woman. Quietly within, she prayed to God for strength. She asked God to help her keep her poise and find the right words.

Just then the lawyer went into a tirade, asking a sarcastic, ruthless question, gesturing in a demeaning way, and shouting loudly.

When he finished his question, she leaned forward, looked him squarely in the eye, and said, "I'm not sure I caught all that. Could you please *scream* that at me again?"

Well, as she said that the jury broke up in laughter, the spectators in the courtroom applauded, the judge chuckled, and the thoroughly squelched lawyer said, "Oh forget it! No more questions."

As the woman stepped down from the witness stand, she quietly prayed, "Thank you, Lord. Thank you for giving me strength!" The meek are those who are steadied by God's presence.

THE MEEK ARE
SELF-GIVING FOR GOD'S SAKE

Arrogant people are brash, haughty, egotistical, and they think only of themselves. But meek people are gentle, kind, self-giving persons who reach out to others in the Spirit of Christ.

43

Robert Fulghum, who wrote *All I Really Need to Know I Learned in Kindergarten*, says that he has placed alongside the mirror in his bathroom a picture of a woman who is *not* his wife—risky business! Every morning as he stands there shaving, he looks at that picture. Now, that impresses me, because I find it necessary to look at my own face when I'm shaving!

The picture shows a small humped-over woman wearing sandals and a blue sari. She is surrounded by important looking people in tuxedos, evening gowns, and the regalia of royalty. It's Mother Teresa, receiving the Nobel Prize! Fulghum said he keeps that picture there to remind him that, more than a president of any nation, more than any pope, more than any chief executive officer of a major corporation, that woman has authority because she is a servant.

Blessed are the meek—those surrendered to God's will, those steadied by God's presence, those who are self-giving for God's sake. They inherit the earth because they are the beloved children of the One who made it.

4
Thirsting for Goodness

Matthew 5:6
Blessed are those who hunger and thirst for righteousness, for they will be filled.

Fourteen years ago, I had the special privilege of helping a young couple adopt a baby. Emil and Dorothy, originally from the Philippines, were thrilled beyond belief when, through Volunteers of America, we were able to find a two-month-old baby boy. They named their new son Christopher, and the very next Sunday morning in church, I had the honor of baptizing him. Emil and Dorothy were delighted and excited.

Not many weeks later, we entered the Christmas season, and on Christmas Eve, Emil called to thank me again for helping them. It was then that he said, "We now owe you a great debt of gratitude which must be repaid."

"No! No!" I protested. "You don't owe me a thing. It was a joy for me to help you adopt Christopher. That is reward enough—and then some!"

Then he said, "But our family has a Christmas gift for your family, and we would be dishonored if you did not accept it."

"Oh, a Christmas gift! That's wonderful!" I responded.

And then he said, "We have a dog for you!"

At that moment, my heart sank. A dog? But that gift turned out to be one of the greatest Christmas gifts we ever received. That little Maltese dog quickly captured our hearts and became a very important member of our family. We named him Datu, which means Prince in the Filipino language—a fitting name because, in princely fashion, he has ruled our household for more than sixteen years now. He weighs only five pounds, and most of that is fluffy white hair, but he is a real heavyweight champion when it comes to love and affection.

Now, there are many fascinating things I could tell you about Datu, but the most remarkable is his incredible passion for his daily walk. He loves to go for a walk! If you just take a step toward the door or act as if you are going to pick up his leash, he goes into the most inspiring routine. His ears perk up. His eyes light up. His tail wags. He runs, he jumps, he celebrates. He does back flips and cartwheels. He cheers, he applauds, he yodels—well, not quite—but you get the picture.

The point is that he lives for that walk! He loves it! And there is absolutely no question about the intensity of that love. He becomes so excited and so animated that you can hardly keep him still long enough to get his leash on. When I see his amazing joy, excitement, anticipation, and enthusiasm, I sometimes find myself thinking that everybody in the world should love something as much as Datu loves his walk!

Let me ask you something. Be honest, now. Do you love anything that much? With that kind of passion and commitment? Is there anything in your life right now that inspires you, excites you, fills you, thrills you, stirs you, motivates you like that? Jesus says that we should be that passionate, that enthusiastic, that fired-up in our pursuit of goodness and righteousness!

Now, that's something to think about, isn't it? Here's how our Lord puts it in the fourth Beatitude: "Blessed are those who hunger and thirst for righteousness, for they will be filled." In other words: "O how happy are those who strive for righteousness!" "O how fulfilled are those who work for justice!" "O how close to God are those who long for goodness!" "O how near to the heart of God are those who crave godliness!"

How is it with you right now? Do you want goodness as much as a starving man wants food? Do you want righteousness as much as someone stranded in the desert wants water? Or have you been looking for life and love and happiness in all the wrong places?

Some years ago one of the young people (a 15-year-old boy) in a church I was serving became stressed-out by problems at school and ran away from home. For four days and nights, we looked for him, but no luck. Finally, on the fifth morning, word came that the police had found him. He was cold, scared, and hungry, but otherwise all right. The officer would have him back home in thirty minutes or so.

I went over to be with the family for his homecoming. When the officer brought him in, there were anxious hugs, tears, apologies, and huge sighs of relief, and then we all went into the kitchen where his mother had fixed breakfast. As we walked in, that teenage boy who had not eaten for four days rushed to the table, and never once thought to bother with the silverware. With both hands, he scooped up the scrambled eggs and began to devour that food like a famished animal. I had never in my life seen anybody that starved for food. Think about that—have you ever been that hungry for righteousness?

When our troops went into Saudi Arabia during the Persian Gulf crisis, there were numerous news stories about the techniques of surviving in the desert. You may remember how they encouraged our soldiers to drink eight gallons of water a day. Eight gallons is a lot of water! If some of those soldiers had been lost in the desert and their water supply had run out, what would they do? They would search for water, long for water, think about water, crave water, pray for water. Have you ever wanted goodness and righteousness in your life as much as those soldiers would want water?

Jesus said, "Blessed are those [close to God are those] who hunger and thirst for righteousness." In his *Gospel of Matthew*, William Barclay is on target when he says, "This beatitude is in reality a question and a challenge. In effect it demands, 'How much do you want goodness? Do you want it as much as a starving man wants food, and as much as a man dying of thirst wants water?' How intense is our desire for goodness?" (p. 95).

Now, of course, the key word here is *righteousness*. What on earth does that word mean? Well, as always, the Scriptures help us. In the Bible, the word *righteousness* is used in three different ways. Let's take a look at these. We may find ourselves, or someone we know, somewhere between the lines.

48

IN THE SCRIPTURES, THE WORD
RIGHTEOUSNESS
MEANS PERSONAL GOODNESS

A few years ago, the bishop asked the new young minister who stood before him a haunting question: "Are you going on to perfection?" Then quickly he added, "If not, where are you going?"

In a sense, that's what this fourth Beatitude says to us: Are you moving toward personal goodness? Are you trying to do better? Are you heading toward a deeper Christian commitment to morality? If not, where are you going?

All of us have seen hitchhikers who stand along the highway holding up signs to indicate where they would like to go, signs that reveal their hoped-for destination. Some are very specific—Dallas, New Orleans, Denver, Little Rock. Others are less exact—Florida, Michigan, Tennessee. Still others are even more general—North, East, South, West. One Christmas season not long ago, a driver saw a young man hitchhiking in Southern California, standing by the highway and holding up a sign that read ANYWHERE.

The truth is that many people go through life like that. They will go anywhere life takes them. Wherever the fads of life, the moods of life, the waves of life take them, they will go—just swept along with no sense of direction. But here in the fourth Beatitude, Jesus reminds us that we need to stop drifting and start moving in the direction of goodness in our personal lives, moving toward morality, pursuing character and ethics and cleanness.

A minister in San Diego was called into the sanctuary early one morning. The custodian wanted him to see a

49

strange offering that had been left on the altar. There were a pair of brown corduroy pants, a belt, a white T-shirt, a pair of tan suede boots, and a note. There were bloodstains on the shirt and on the note. The note said: "Please listen to God." It was signed, and there was a phone number.

The minister dialed the number. A nineteen-year-old young man answered and told his story. He had run away from home and had been wandering in a wasteland of drugs, drifting from one place to another, getting into all kinds of trouble and involved in all kinds of sordid behavior. The night before, he had hit bottom. There had been a struggle on the streets, a fight, and an almost fatal beating. After making sure the victim of his uncontrolled assault would be all right in the emergency room of a nearby hospital, this young man came to the church, found an unlocked door, and went into the sanctuary.

He stayed there all night, crying, praying, and pondering. He asked God to forgive him and show him the way to go. All at once the presence of God became very real. He knew God was there. He felt God's forgiveness. A wonderful peace came. He committed himself to follow Christ. He determined to make right the things he had messed up. He felt fresh and clean, like a new man. To symbolize his new life and new commitment, he had put on some new clothes he had with him in his bedroll and had left the others as a kind of offering, giving God his old life. He walked out the door a new person with a new vision, a new hope, a new life, a new direction.

Why did he come to the church? Why did he pray all night? Why did he plead for forgiveness? Why did he make that new commitment? Why did he put on new clothes? Because he was hungry for God, thirsty for goodness. When he came to his senses, like the prodigal son, he wanted to come home to God. He realized that his soul was starving. He wanted to do better and be better. How is it with you and me? How much do we want the righteousness of personal goodness?

IN THE SCRIPTURES, THE WORD *RIGHTEOUSNESS* ALSO MEANS SOCIAL JUSTICE

Many years ago, a young lawyer made a trip to New Orleans. He saw something happening there that broke his heart and turned his stomach—a slave auction. Slaves had been brought in by boat and were being sold to the highest bidders. The sights and sounds of that moment were locked forever in the mind of that young lawyer. Children were crying, women were screaming, men were struggling helplessly against their shackles as families were torn apart, the members probably never to see one another again. Human beings were being treated like animals. It was a cruel, sordid business, and as that young lawyer watched the ugliness and the inhumanity with tears in his eyes, he said, "This is wrong! Terribly wrong! And if I ever get a chance to strike a blow against this, I will do it with all my strength!"

Do you know who that young lawyer was? His name was Abraham Lincoln, and when in time his opportunity to right that wrong came, he stood tall and struck the blow for justice. A part of our calling as a church is to be the "conscience of society" and stand tall for social justice. All through the Bible we see it. Moses, Amos,

Isaiah, Elijah, the apostle Paul, and especially Jesus—all committed themselves not only to personal goodness, but also to social justice. How is it with you and me? How much do we want the righteousness of social justice?

IN THE SCRIPTURES, THE WORD *RIGHTEOUSNESS* ALSO MEANS RIGHT RELATIONSHIPS

I read recently about a man who prayed, "O God, use me any way you desire, but especially in the advisory capacity." Well, the truth is that God doesn't want us in the advisory capacity. He wants us in the *relational* capacity.

In the original Greek New Testament, the word for "righteousness" is dikaiosuna, and it literally means, "be set right with God and other people."

This is one of the major themes of the Bible. The great Command is to love God and people, and the best way to express our love for God is to show love for God's children. The prophets said it, and so did Paul. And so did Jesus. But so often we forget this, don't we? Too often, we ignore God, and too often we hurt each other.

Some years ago in the north, a little girl was lost in the woods. It was wintertime, snowing, sleeting, and bitterly cold. Hundreds of people combed the forest, desperately searching for the little girl. Time was of the essence. They knew she couldn't survive long in that freezing weather. For hours they looked, but no luck. Finally, the searchers came up with the idea of joining hands, so that they could walk through the forest in a single line.

They tried it, and in less than fifteen minutes they found her! But it was too late. She had died from cold and exposure.

In the hush of that awful moment, someone said, "Why, O why didn't we join hands sooner?" Sometimes when I see the troubles and conflicts in the world, I think about that. Why, O why, can't we join hands?

This is what it means to hunger and thirst for righteousness—to strive energetically for personal goodness, to stand tall enthusiastically for social justice, and to join hands eagerly with God and other people in loving relationships.

5
Mercy, the Virtue That Shines

Matthew 5:7
Blessed are the merciful,
for they will receive mercy.

During the War Between the States, a young teenage boy enlisted to be a soldier for the Union army. But he was not ready. He was much too young, and when the time came for his first encounter with the enemy, he became terrified and ran away. He was caught, arrested, judged guilty of desertion and sentenced to be shot by a firing squad.

His parents wrote a letter to President Abraham Lincoln, pleading for mercy, pleading for a pardon for their young son. Touched by their letter, President Lincoln called for the facts and when he realized the situation, he overruled the death sentence and granted the teenager a full presidential pardon.

In his official statement explaining his action, Mr. Lincoln wrote these words: "Over the years . . . I have observed that it does not do a boy much good to shoot him!"

On another occasion some months later, as the Civil War was winding down and it was obvious that the

Union would win, someone asked President Lincoln how he would treat the southerners after the war was over.

He answered, "Like they had never been away."

"But Mr. President," the questioner protested, "aren't we supposed to destroy our enemies?"

I love Abraham Lincoln's response: "Don't we destroy our enemies when we make them our friends?"

That is the quality of mercy, and that gracious, forgiving spirit is one of the things that has so endeared Abraham Lincoln to America and made him one of the great leaders of history. He lived out the truth of the fifth Beatitude: "Blessed are the merciful, for they will receive mercy."

Of all the Beatitudes, this one is probably the most appealing and the easiest for us to understand. Some of the Beatitudes, to be honest, seem a bit obscure and puzzling until we study them more closely. For example, at first glance we are not sure what it means to be "poor in spirit." We wonder sometimes if it is really blessed to "mourn." We want to know just how the "pure in heart" will see God. We have to be convinced that "the meek" will inherit the earth. And we don't find much joy in being "persecuted."

But when it comes to mercy, we all smile and nod our heads. There is something really quite beautiful about the picture of mercy, and one reason we like it so much is because we need it so much. We need to receive it, and we need to pass it on.

Mercy is a virtue that shines. We hold it in high regard. We endorse it, affirm it, applaud it, and with good reason. That reason becomes so very clear when we consider the alternatives—vengeance, bitterness, grudges, anger, hate, resentment, vindictiveness, hostility—all these are spiritual poisons that will contaminate our spirits and devastate our souls.

The hateful unforgiving spirit does not make a pretty picture. Hate is like a spiritual narcotic that slowly but surely imprisons and destroys the user, like the raging fire that annihilates the arsonist. Hate is like the mad scientist who methodically builds a bomb to use on others, only to have it blow up in his hands.

There is no question about it. Mercy is so much more attractive and so much more productive than grudges and hatred and vengeance and vindictiveness. But you know, I think the reason we like mercy so much is because it reminds us of God. There is no quality in this world more God-like than mercy. God is merciful. That is the good news of our faith. And God wants us to be merciful people. That is the spirit of our faith.

One of Shakespeare's most beloved quotes is about mercy: "The quality of mercy is not strained; it droppeth as the gentle rain from heaven upon the place beneath; it is twice blest; it blesseth those that give and those that receive."

Some years ago I saw a television commercial for a headache powder that amused me. A dignified man dressed in a white medical jacket said in a reassuring, confident voice: "Our headache powder is best because it is a combination of ingredients." But he never said what the ingredients were! He only said, "It is a combination of ingredients."

I always wanted to shout back at the TV, "What isn't?" *Everything* is a combination of ingredients!

Interestingly, Jesus talked about the "ingredients" of mercy. He equated *mercy* with spiritual maturity. For example, in Matthew 5:48 He says "Be perfect as your heavenly Father is perfect." In other words, "Be spiritually mature as your heavenly Father is spiritually mature." In Luke 6, Jesus says almost the same thing: "Be merciful, just as your Father is merciful." The point is clear: Mercy is one of the highest expressions of spiritual maturity. It is one of the most God-like qualities in all the world. "O how near to the heart of God are those who imitate God's merciful spirit."

One of the most powerful parables of Jesus makes the point dramatically, the parable of the unmerciful servant, in Matthew 18.

Simon Peter has just asked Jesus, "How often should I forgive?"

Jesus answers by telling a story about a servant who owes his king $10 million. He can't pay it; the debt is too great. He begs for mercy. The king hears the man's story and his heart goes out to the man. And amazingly, the king forgives the whole debt! Relieved, overjoyed, set free, the forgiven man leaves the palace. But as he walks out, he sees a fellow servant who owes him $20.

He grabs his debtor by the throat and says, "Pay me the $20 you owe me! Pay me right now!"

The fellow servant falls down and pleads for mercy, for more time to make good the small debt. But the unmerciful servant refuses and has the man thrown into prison. Can you imagine this? The one who has just been forgiven a debt of $10 million has the man who owes him $20 arrested and put in jail! When the king hears about this, he is livid, and he has the unmerciful servant cast into prison.

This story shows us that God is merciful and quick to

58

forgive, and God wants us to live in that gracious spirit. We are expected to imitate God's merciful ways. We have been forgiven so much. Through the sacrificial love of Jesus Christ, we have been forgiven an enormous, astounding debt! How could we not pass that forgiveness on to others? God is merciful toward us, and God wants us to be merciful in our dealings with one another.

As I have studied this fifth Beatitude, I have found myself asking, "What are the key ingredients that combine to make up the quality of mercy?" Of course, there are many. But for now, let me ask you to try these three on for size.

A KEY INGREDIENT OF MERCY IS
EMPATHY

One of the most powerful words in the Old Testament is the Hebrew word *chesedh*, the word for "mercy." It means lovingkindness. It means to be tenderhearted, so full of empathy that we can get right inside other people's skins, can stand in their shoes until we see things with their eyes, think with their minds, feel with their hearts. And that is the starting place for mercy. A merciful person is by definition an empathetic person who can feel the pain that others are feeling.

In the Chicago area a few years ago, a fifteen-year-old boy became very ill. His temperature went up to 105. He was rushed to the hospital. Blood tests revealed the bad news. He had leukemia. The doctors were very frank as they told him what to expect—long hospital stays, endless tests and treatments, and three years of chemotherapy.

The boy became very discouraged. His family called a local flower shop to order some flowers to brighten his hospital room. They explained to the young salesclerk that the boy had been told that he has leukemia, and they hoped the arrangement would be especially attractive.

"Oh," said the young salesclerk, "I understand. I will add some fresh cut flowers to brighten it up. I know just what to do."

And when the flowers arrived, they were indeed beautiful. Strangely, there were two cards in the envelope attached to the arrangement—one from Douglas' family and one from Laura Bradley. But who was Laura Bradley? No one recognized that name. They thought it was a mistake until Douglas read the card aloud: "I took your order. I work at the flower shop. I had leukemia when I was seven years old. I'm twenty-two now. Good luck. My heart goes out to you."

Douglas' face lit up. For the first time since he entered the hospital, he had been inspired. He had talked to many doctors and nurses, but this card was the thing that made him believe he might beat the disease.

This story was reported in the *Chicago Tribune* by syndicated columnist Bob Greene. Mr. Greene said that when he spoke to the salesclerk who had written the note to Doug, she said: "When [they] told me that he had leukemia, I felt tears coming to my eyes. It reminded me of when I first learned that I had it. I realized what he must be going through. I wanted him to know that you really can get better. So I wrote the card and slipped it into the envelope. I didn't tell anyone. I haven't been working here very long and I was afraid I might get into trouble."

"It's funny," wrote Bob Greene. "Doug was in a hospital filled with millions of dollars of the most sophisticated medical equipment. He was being treated by expert doctors and nurses with medical training totaling hundreds of years. But it was a salesclerk in a flower shop, a woman making $170 a week, who, by taking the time to care, and being willing to go with what her heart told her to do, gave Douglas hope . . . and the will to carry on. The human spirit can be an amazing thing . . . and sometimes you encounter it at it's very best when you aren't even looking."

Empathy is indeed a beautiful thing. It is the launching pad for the quality of mercy. It's one of mercy's key ingredients. God is a merciful and empathetic God who wants us to be merciful and empathetic people.

A SECOND KEY INGREDIENT OF MERCY IS *GENEROSITY*

Merciful people are generous people, people who are willing to go out on a limb and even to sacrifice for others.

A number of years ago in a mental institution outside Boston, a young girl known as Little Annie was locked in a dungeon. The dungeon was the only place, said the doctors, for those who were hopelessly insane. In Little Annie's case, they saw no hope at all, so she was consigned to a living death in that small cage which received little light and even less hope.

About that time, an elderly nurse was nearing retirement. She felt there was hope for all of God's children, so she decided to try to help Little Annie. She began taking her lunch into the dungeon and eating outside Little Annie's cage. She wanted to somehow communicate love and hope to the little girl. In many ways, Little Annie was like a wild animal. On occasion, she would violently attack anyone who came into her cage. At other times, she would completely ignore the person.

When the elderly nurse started visiting her, Little Annie gave no indication that she was even aware of her presence. One day the nurse brought some brownies and left them just outside the cage, but reachable. Little Annie gave no hint that she knew they were there, but when the nurse returned the next day, the brownies were gone. From that time forward, the nurse would leave brownies or some treat each day.

Soon Annie began to communicate with the woman and they became friends. Then the doctors noticed an amazing improvement in Little Annie, and they took her out of the dungeon. They moved her upstairs and began to work with her. And over time, Little Annie became totally well. This "hopeless" case was completely whole and bright and sane. They told her she could go home. But Little Annie did not wish to leave. She chose to stay to help others.

Later, however, she did leave. She went out to help another little girl who also was having a hard time. Annie went to help a little girl who also was considered a hopeless case. The name of the troubled girl Annie went to help was Helen Keller. Little Annie's real name was Anne Sullivan!

When our son, Jeff, was born some years ago, I can remember standing in the corridor of the hospital, looking in the nursery window, my nose pressed against the glass, admiring our new little boy.

A woman came over and said, "Is that your baby?"

I proudly answered, "Yes!"

And then she said, "Isn't that something! He looks just like a little person!"

I thought to myself: "He is! That's exactly what he is—a little person!"

The key to being merciful is just that—to see everyone we meet, whatever the age or station, as a person, a person of value and integrity, a person for whom Christ came—and to look at them in the spirit of Christ, with generous and gracious eyes.

A THIRD KEY INGREDIENT OF MERCY IS *FORGIVENESS*

Some years ago in New England, a woman became angry with a pastor and began to harass him in every way she could. She started false rumors, called him ugly names, wrote vicious letters, threatened him, made false accusations. After several months, the woman moved to another city and not long afterward, was converted to Christ.

Part of the process of her conversion was to realize the terrible wrong she had done and all the pain, suffering, and embarrassment she had inflicted on that pastor in New England. Finally she sat down and wrote him a long letter, explaining what had happened to her and how deeply she regretted what she had done. She begged him to accept her apology. She mailed the letter and two days later, she received a telegram from that pastor. It contained three words: "Forgiven! Forgotten! Forever!" Isn't that something? Merciful people are quick to forgive.

Someone once gave me a Christmas card that says it all. It's titled "God Sent Us a Savior" and continued with these powerful lines:

> If our greatest need had been information, God would have sent us an Educator.
>
> If our greatest need had been technology, God would have sent us a Scientist.
>
> If our greatest need had been money, God would have sent us an Economist.
>
> If our greatest need had been pleasure, God would have sent us an Entertainer.
>
> But our greatest need was forgiveness, so God sent us a Savior—
>
> A Savior who came to forgive us—and then sends us out to be his agents of forgiveness!

Empathy, generosity, forgiveness—these are the key ingredients combined in the incredible quality of *mercy*. "O how near to the heart of God are those who receive God's mercy, accept God's mercy in faith, and pass God's mercy on to others."

6
The Dangers of Mask-wearing

Matthew 5:8
*Blessed are the pure in heart,
for they will see God.*

Sometimes on festive occasions we wear costumes and masks to celebrate in a special way. We wear these masks for three reasons:

1. So we can pretend to be something we are not.
2. So we can disguise who we really are.
3. So we can separate ourselves from everybody else.

Where I grew up, we used to call these masks false faces. We wear masks for parties and celebrations, but for some people mask-wearing is an everyday affair. They wear "false faces" continually—pretending to be something they are not, trying to disguise who they really are, setting themselves apart from everybody else.

When Jesus came into the world, he saw people wearing masks, and it bothered him. Of course, the most notorious "mask-wearers" of Jesus' day were the religious leaders—the Pharisees and the Sadducees. They wore the mask of outward purity, a mask that said to everybody, "Look at me! See how clean and pure and godly I am. See my good works! Aren't you impressed? See how I keep the Law. Don't come too near me now, for I am holier-than-thou!"

But all that pompous, pious talk, was like a false face, an artificial appearance. They looked good outwardly, but inwardly, their hearts were made of stone. They talked loudly of goodness, but they kicked sand in the faces of the hurting people around them. They kept the letter of the Law, but missed the message of mercy and love. They were so busy holding their "I'm better than you" mask in place, they had no time or energy left over for compassion.

Jesus saw right through their pretensions and disguises, and he had strong words for them: "Woe to you, scribes and Pharisees, hypocrites! For you are like whitewashed tombs, which . . . inside are full of the bones of the dead" (Matt. 23:27). Those are tough words, to be sure, but Jesus wanted to emphasize dramatically the importance of the inner life. It's what's inside that counts! That's what he says in this sixth Beatitude: "Blessed are the pure in heart, for they will see God."

In other words: Don't be pretentious! Don't be fake. Don't be artificial! Don't be holier-than-thou! Don't be hypocritical! Don't make a show of religion and miss the message! Be genuine and honest and real within. Give God your heart.

When I study the Bible, I usually read with a pencil in my hand to underscore special phrases or words I think need to be stressed or emphasized or internalized. If Jesus were to do that with this sixth Beatitude, I think he would underscore the words *in heart*. "Blessed are the pure in heart." When Jesus spoke of the heart, he didn't mean just the emotions. He meant the inner life, the total personality—the ideas, the attitudes, the motives, the commitments within.

When we in the church today say, "Give God your heart," that's what we mean. "Give God your inner life." "Give God the real you." In *The Applause of Heaven*, Max Lucado writes:

> The heart is the center of the spiritual life. . . . That is why the state of the heart is so critical. What's the state of yours?
>
> When someone barks at you, do you bark back or bite your tongue? That depends on the state of your heart.
>
> When your schedule is too tight or your to-do list too long, do you lose your cool or keep it? That depends on the state of your heart.
>
> When you are offered a morsel of gossip marinated in slander, do you turn it down or pass it on? That depends on the state of your heart. . . .
>
> The state of your heart dictates whether you harbor a grudge or give grace, seek self-pity or seek Christ, drink human misery or taste God's mercy.
>
> No wonder, then, the wise man begs, "Above all else, guard your heart."
>
> David's prayer should be ours: "Create in me a pure heart, O God."
>
> And Jesus' statement rings true: "Blessed are the pure in heart, for they shall see God." (p. 121)

Let me bring this a bit closer to home by suggesting some key qualities that describe those who are pure in heart.

THE PURE IN HEART ARE SINCERE

The pure in heart are those who are absolutely genuine in their desire to serve and love God. They are authentic and single-minded in their devotion to God and in their friendships with other people. The pure in heart are not two-faced. They don't wear masks. They don't pretend to be something they are not. They don't disguise who they really are. They don't act "holier than thou." They are not artificial or superficial or hypocritical.

The pure in heart are genuine in motive, sincere in worship, authentic through and through. They are genuine in their thanksgivings and in their service. They are sincere in praising God and in giving compliments to other people. They are trustworthy in friendship and solid in Christian living. In other words, they practice what they preach. Blessed are the pure in heart, for they are sincere.

THE PURE IN HEART
ARE THOSE WHO LOVE

Gary Smalley is one of America's best selling authors and most popular speakers on human relationships. In one of his seminars, he does a very interesting thing. He pulls out an old violin. It's obviously an antique and also obviously in need of repair. It doesn't look like it could be worth much at all. In fact, it really looks like a piece of junk.

He holds it up high for all to see, and then he says, "Do you have any idea how much this violin is worth?

68

This may surprise you, but it's actually worth $800,000 to a million dollars, because if you look through the opening on the face of the violin, you can see inside some very special words: '1722 Stradivarius.'"

When he says that, the audience goes "AHHHH!"

Then he goes on, "If you will honor other people like that, it will change your life. It's the greatest relationship principle I know of. Watch your attitudes and feelings change as you become skilled at honoring those around you." He adds, "I want you to go home and write on the forehead of your mate the word 'Stradivarius'. Write on the foreheads of your children 'Stradivarius'—because they are much more valuable than any violin."

Now, Jesus would like that counsel. As a matter of fact, he would enlarge it. He would say: "Write the word Stradivarius on the forehead of every single person you meet. Honor them. Value them. Esteem them. Appreciate them. Love them."

The pure in heart are those who love. They give themselves in complete devotion to God. And they treat others with respect. They love God with heart, soul, mind, and strength, and they love other people in self-giving sacrificial ways.

The pure in heart are those who love by giving of themselves completely. They give themselves in complete devotion to God, expecting nothing in return. They love God with heart, soul, mind, and strength, and other people in self-giving, sacrificial ways. The pure in heart are those who reach out in love to other people and up in love to God. Blessed are the pure in heart. They are sincere, and they know how to love.

THE PURE IN HEART ARE CHILDLIKE

The pure in heart are those who are completely guileless, open and honest and trusting. Jesus put it like this: "Whoever does not receive the kingdom of God as a little child will never enter it" (Mark 10:15). Someone else put it this way: "Every person under seven and over seventy is completely honest. They say what they feel. They are guileless and transparent. They wear no masks. They are what they are. They are genuine."

My friend Dorothy Cardwell, a talented and dedicated teacher of children for many years, once wrote this devotional about the beauty of childlikeness:

> First of all, childlikeness is perfect trust. Knowing the security of a parent's love, a child finds it a simple and natural step to accept with complete confidence the love and care of the heavenly Father.
>
> Second, childlikeness is wide-eyed wonder. Adults so often pass by and fail to see the feathers of a bird, the color of an autumn leaf, the wild flower in a field, or the shape of a cloud. How glad we must make the heart of our Creator when we recapture the wide-eyed wonder that is so special in little children.
>
> Third, childlikeness is eager expectancy. A child wastes no precious moments bemoaning what happened yesterday. Like children, let us be glad for the challenge and blessing each new day brings.
>
> Fourth, childlikeness is a lack of pretense. Only when we strip away our self-righteousness and see ourselves as we truly are can God make us what he wants us to be.

Blessed are the pure in heart. They are sincere. They know how to love. And they are beautifully childlike with wonder and trust and honesty.

THE PURE IN HEART ARE IN A RIGHT RELATIONSHIP WITH GOD

When people are pure in heart, they have experienced the cleansing that only God can give. God is the "heart purifier." You can count on that. The One who made us is the One who knows just how to purify us—from the inside out.

Now, let me ask you a very important question. What do you really want in life? What do you really want life to grant you? Many answers to that have been given down through the ages.

Ruell Howe suggests that what we really want in life is to be at-one with somebody and to have somebody be at-one with us. What he is suggesting is what Augustine said a long time ago—that we are hungering and thirsting to be in communion with God. Augustine put it like this: "Thou has made us for Thyself, O God, and our hearts are restless 'til they find their rest in Thee."

In Thomas Costain's famous novel, *The Silver Chalice*, when Basil, the main character first sees the cup of the Last Supper, he sees nothing special. To him, it just looks like an old dented silver mug. It looks ordinary, cheap, even worthless, and he really doesn't see what all the fuss is about. But then Basil is converted! He becomes a Christian. He gives his heart to God. He accepts Christ as his Savior and Lord, and he becomes pure in heart.

Then he looks again at that cup, and this time he sees a magnificent chalice, brilliant with the light of heaven. The cup has not changed in any way, but Basil has changed. His heart has been touched, and his eyes have been "Christ-ed." And now when he looks at that sacred cup, he sees the most beautiful thing he has ever laid his eyes on. He sees the "good news" of God's gracious acceptance of him. He sees the sacrifice of Christ, the blood of Christ, the love of Christ.

Before, he was blind to it, but now Christ has purified his heart and opened his eyes. That's the way it works, and that's what this sixth beatitude is all about. Blessed are the pure in heart, those whose hearts have been cleansed and changed by the indwelling Christ, for they see God everywhere.

7
The Best Thing We Can Do for God

Matthew 5:9
Blessed are the peacemakers,
for they will be called children of God.

I recently read about a four-year-old boy who was in the back seat of the family car, eating an apple.

"Daddy," said the child, "why is my apple turning brown?"

His father explained, "Because after you ate the outer skin off, the meat of the apple came into contact with the air, which caused it to oxidize, changing its molecular structure, and thus turning it into a different color."

There was a long silence, and the little boy asked softly, "Daddy, are you talking to me?"

Sometimes that's the way we feel when we read the Beatitudes. We hear these strange sounding words—blessed are the poor in spirit, the meek, the persecuted, those who mourn—and we find ourselves wanting to cry out, like the little boy, "Lord, are you talking to me? I mean, you don't really want me to do these things, do you? You're not really talking to me, are you, Lord?" Well, of course!

73

The answer is a resounding Yes! God is talking to us in all the Beatitudes, and in this seventh Beatitude, God is saying specifically to us, "Yes, you! I want you to be a peacemaker. There is nothing in the world you can do that will please me more. Peacemaking is what it's all about. It is the most God-like thing you can do!"

Peacemaking is the very height of spiritual maturity. Childish people want to fight. Spiritually mature people want to heal. Childish people build walls. Spiritually mature people build bridges. Childish people resent. Spiritually mature people reconcile.

A strong indicator of the sacred significance of peacemaking is found in the last phrase: "They will be called children of God." The phrase "children of God" is dramatically important, because in biblical times, there was an economy of speech; there were not enough words to go around, not enough words to cover every situation. This was especially true of descriptive adjectives, so they would use such phrases as "child of ____" or "son of ____" or "daughter of ____," followed by an abstract noun.

For example, if you wanted to say, "That man is a very honest man," you would say that he is a "son of honesty." Or if a woman became noted for her kindness, she would be referred to as a "daughter of kindness."

James and John were called the sons of thunder, and Barnabas was the "son of encouragement." So when we read that the peacemakers will be called "children of God," it means, "Blessed are the peacemakers, for they are doing a God-like work." Nothing is more Godly than the act of peacemaking. If you want to "make happy" the heart of God, live in that spirit! Be a

74

reconciler. Imitate God's redemptive, peacemaking ways!

One of the things that fascinates me about baseball is the way the coaches position their players on the field. When a power hitter comes up, they move them in the direction of his power, or if a spray hitter comes to bat, they move the players in the other direction. And sometimes they play them straight away. If the coaches expect the hitter to bunt, they pull the players up close; they place them midway when they hope to turn a double play. In the latter innings, they move everybody way back to avoid an extra base-hit.

Coaches will tell you convincingly that close games often are won or lost just by the positioning of the players. A particular play can succeed or fail because of the placement of the players. It's true in all sports. Positioning is all-important. It is tremendously important, too, in the game of life. And in this seventh Beatitude, Jesus is saying to us, "Here's your position! Go into life as peacemakers! Let that be your stance! Let that be your attitude, your commitment! Take the position of peacemakers!"

Over the years, scholars have come at this seventh Beatitude from three different directions. Some have said it has to do with the Hebrew word *shalom*. *Shalom* means "wholeness, fullness, everything you need to make life good." So in that context, this Beatitude could be paraphrased as: "Blessed are those who work to improve the quality of life for everyone and make this world a better place to live."

This is what Abraham Lincoln meant when he said, "I would like it to be said of me that I always pulled up a weed and planted a flower where I thought a flower would grow."

Other scholars have suggested that this Beatitude has to do with *inner peace*—peace within, serenity in our hearts and souls. Still others say that this Beatitude challenges us to work harder on *our relationships with others.* That's what it's all about, they say—being in a right relationship with other people. I'm sure it means some of all of these. I'm equally sure that the real peacemakers are those who have the following three important qualities.

PEACEMAKERS ARE PATIENT

When we study the Scriptures, we realize pretty quickly that one of God's greatest qualities is God's patience. Again and again, God patiently forgives. God knows our weakness, sees our sins, and is very much aware of our clay feet. Yet with amazing patience, God keeps on forgiving us, loving us, encouraging us. This seventh Beatitude challenges us to imitate God's patient ways.

Ruth Graham, wife of evangelist Billy Graham, has decided what she wants on her tombstone. It's not what you would expect at all, but a most unusual statement indeed. She saw it one day on a road sign when she and her husband were driving down an interstate highway. They had gone through several miles of road construction, had to slow down, were reduced to single lanes of traffic, and had to make short detours here and there. Finally they came to the end of the construction—and there Ruth Graham saw the sign that caught her attention.

Pointing to it, she said to her husband, "Look! That's what I want on my tombstone!" At first he didn't get it, but when it began to dawn on him, he smiled. The sign read: END OF CONSTRUCTION. THANKS FOR YOUR PATIENCE.

Actually, that would be a pretty accurate summary for the lives of all of us, wouldn't it? We all have feet of clay, we all have our shortcomings and foibles and inadequacies, we all mess up from time to time. Every now and then, we blow it, we all stumble and fall. All of us are still under construction, and we all need God and other people to be patient with us. So why not just recognize that, and turn that coin over and be patient with other people! Why not take that stance? Why not be a bridge-builder? Why not be an avid agent of reconciliation? Why not imitate the gracious patience of God? Why not be a patient peacemaker? It's a God-like thing to do.

PEACEMAKERS ARE LOVING

Disrespect for others is not a pretty picture—whether it's a husband or wife giving a spouse a hard time, or a man pushing people out of the way so he can get on an airplane first, or a child calling her mother an ugly name in a cafeteria line, or insecure people who try to force their way of life and their ideas on everybody they meet, or a military tyrant aggressively and cruelly invading another country. Hostility toward others is not a pretty picture! It is ungodly behavior, and peacemakers don't act that way!

Some time ago the church I serve lost one of our finest

members. His name was George. Everybody loved George because he was a peacemaker. He had a big heart and a wonderful sense of humor. He used to say that he was "so tenderhearted that he cried at supermarket openings"! He was deeply loved at church and at the hospital where he worked, for he was kind and respectful toward every person he met.

A few days before George died, the president of the hospital stopped by his hospital room. They had a nice visit. As the president left, one of the janitors came in to see George. They, too, had a good visit.

When the janitor left, one of George's children said to him, "Dad, did you realize that you treated the president of the hospital and the janitor just alike?"

George smiled and said with a chuckle, "Let me ask you something. If the president left for two weeks and the janitor left for two weeks, which one do you think would be missed the most?"

And then George said to his children, "Come over here. Let me show you something I carry in my pocket all the time. Even when I mow the lawn, I have these two things in my pocket." With that, he pulled out his pocket cross and his golden-rule marble.

He said, "On the cross are written these words: 'God Loves You'; and on the marble are these words: 'Do unto Others as You Would Have Them Do unto You.' The cross reminds me of how deeply God loves me, and the marble reminds me of how deeply God wants me to love others."

What George was saying was this: "This is my position, my life-stance, symbolized by a little silver cross and a red Golden Rule marble. I just want to let the love of God flow through me and out to others."

That's what it means to be a peacemaker, and that's what St. Francis meant when he prayed, "Lord, make me an instrument of thy peace. Where there is hatred, let me sow love, where there is injury . . . pardon."

PEACEMAKERS ARE CHRISTLIKE

How do we find the spirit of Christ? How do we find what the apostle Paul called "the mind of Christ"? Fred Craddock tells a beautiful story that helps us with the answer.

Dr. Craddock had been a visiting preacher in the church of an older couple we will call Nora and Frank, and Nora invited him home for Sunday lunch. Her husband hadn't made it to church that day because he had shingles. When they arrived, Frank was sitting in a rocking chair in front of the fireplace. Frank was in his 80's. Nora introduced Dr. Craddock and Frank and then went into the kitchen to prepare lunch.

Dr. Craddock spoke first: "Well, Frank, how are you feeling?"

"Terrible."

"I understand you have the shingles."

"Yep! The shingles. It's awful. Don't see how I can stand it much longer."

"You still have the pain?"

"O yeah. It's constant pain."

"Well, how long have you had this, Frank?"

"Oh, I don't know. I've had it ever since last October or November, I don't remember which." Then he shouted, "Nora! Was it October or November?"

She called out, "November."

And Frank said, "Since last November."

79

Later at the lunch table, Dr. Craddock asked, "Nora, how in the world did you know what he was talking about when he yelled out about October or November? How did you know what he meant?"

Nora just smiled and said, "Dr. Craddock, we've been married for 53 years!" Wasn't that beautiful? She just knew—because she was "tuned in" to Frank.

If we live with somebody in a loving, trusting relationship over a period of time, we begin to think like that other person thinks. If we spend enough quality time with Christ, we take on the mind of Christ. If we spend enough time with the Son of God, we become real children of God. If we spend enough time with the Prince of Peace, we will become peacemakers!

8
Come What May, We Can Trust God

Matthew 5:10-12
Blessed are those who are persecuted for righteousness'
sake, for theirs is the kingdom of heaven.
Blessed are you when people revile you and persecute you
and utter all kinds of evil against you falsely on my
account. Rejoice and be glad, for your reward is great in
heaven, for in the same way they persecuted the prophets
who were before you.

Search Institute in Minneapolis, Minnesota, recently conducted a fascinating research project in which they surveyed more than 11,000 people from 561 different Protestant congregations. One question they asked was this: What constitutes mature faith? What are the marks of genuine spiritual maturity?

From that study, they concluded that spiritually mature people always seem to exhibit eight very special qualities:

1. They trust in God's saving grace, and they believe firmly in the humanity and divinity of Jesus.

2. They feel good about themselves; they experience a sense of personal well-being, security, and peace.

3. They integrate faith and life, seeing work, family,

81

social relationships, and political choices as part of one's religious life.

4. They seek spiritual growth through study, reflection, prayer, and discussion with others.

5. They seek to be part of a community of believers in which people give witness to their faith, and support and nourish one another.

6. They hold life-affirming values, including commitment to racial and gender equality, affirmation of cultural and religious diversity, and a personal sense of responsibility for the welfare of others.

7. They advocate social and global change to bring about greater peace and justice.

8. They serve humanity consistently and passionately, through acts of love and justice.

It's significant to note that five of these eight characteristics involve seeing Christ in our neighbors and knowing that in serving them, we are serving him. Remember how Jesus said it in Matthew 25:40: "Truly I tell you just as you did it to one of the least of these . . . you did it to me."

It's also interesting to note how closely these Search Institute marks of mature faith resemble the Beatitudes. Matthew 5 is not a list of clever proverbs or a compilation of unrelated, independent sayings. Rather, what we have in the Beatitudes is a step-by-step outline of the faith pilgrimage, a chronological description of the way the spiritual life unfolds, how it develops and matures:

1. First, we are poor in spirit—that is, we humbly recognize how much we need God.

2. Second, we mourn our sins.

82

3. Third, in meekness, we offer ourselves unconditionally as God's servants; we commit our lives totally
to God.

4. Next, we want to learn the faith, to grow
spiritually; we hunger and thirst for righteousness.

5. Then we go out into the world to live the faith in
the spirit of mercy . . .

6. . . . and the spirit of genuineness, being authentic—not being hypocritical, but pure in heart.

7. Finally, we come to the height of spiritual
maturity. In the spirit of God, we become peacemakers,
reconcilers.

8. Then Jesus adds a P.S.: "Oh, by the way," he says,
"if you do these things—if you live the Beatitudes out
there in the day-to-day world—you may well be
persecuted. People may turn against you. They may
give you a hard time, but don't be afraid, because I am
with you. I will protect you. I will see you through."

RELIGIOUS PERSECUTION

Did you notice that this last Beatitude is three times
longer than the other seven? Each of the others is
covered in just one verse, but this last one takes up
three full verses, a whole paragraph—and with good
reason. The early Christians lived daily under the threat
of persecution. A constant, fearsome cloud was always
hanging over them. It took incredible courage to be a
Christian in those early days. Jesus knew that those first
Christians would be persecuted, so he didn't mince
words. He laid it on the line!

Jesus was so honest. He never left people in doubt

about what would happen to them if they chose to follow him. He made it clear that he had come "not to make life easy, but to make people great." And indeed, those early Christians did need to be greatly committed to their faith to survive the persecutions. Many of them lost their jobs. Many of them were ostracized socially. Some of them were kicked out of their homes, cast out by their own families because they had accepted Christ.

And there was slander. They were accused of cannibalism. The words of the Lord's Supper—"This is my body. . . . This is my blood"—were twisted into a totally false story that Christians were sacrificing babies and eating their flesh. It was cruel gossip, malicious slander. In addition, their weekly meeting was called the Agape or Love Feast, and you can imagine what the world did with that! Those early Christians were scandalously accused of sexual immorality. It was all a lie, but the early Christians had to live with these kinds of false accusations.

POLITICAL PERSECUTION

But the great ground of persecution was in fact political. The Roman Empire was vast and wide, and the rulers needed a way to unify the empire, to hold the people together. So over time, the way that emerged was emperor worship. Worship of the emperor became compulsory, and that was a real problem for those early Christians.

At least once a year, the people had to burn incense in homage to Caesar. They had to bow down and say, "Caesar is Lord." And that is precisely what the

84

Christians refused to do. For them, Jesus Christ was the Lord. They would not compromise on that. They would not give that title to anyone else. Confronted with the choice, Caesar or Christ?, they unflinchingly chose Christ. The earliest Christian creed was only three words long—Jesus is Lord—and when the early Christians said that, they also meant that Caesar wasn't. And that unwavering loyalty to Christ got them in a whole lot of trouble.

Some were burned at the stake or fed to the lions, and those were the more kindly deaths. William Barclay, in *The Gospel of Matthew*, gives this graphic description:

> Nero wrapped the Christians in pitch and set them alight, and used them as living torches to light his gardens. He sewed them in the skins of wild animals and set his hunting dogs upon them to tear them to death. They were tortured on the rack; they were scraped with pincers; molten lead was poured hissing upon them. . . . These things are not pleasant to think about, but these are the things a man had to be prepared for, if he took his stand with Christ. (p. 112).

PERSONAL PERSECUTION

From the beginning, the followers of Christ have been persecuted for righteousness' sake. They have been reviled, attacked, slandered, and falsely accused. And sadly, it's still happening. It's more subtle now, but it's still there. All you need do to stir some people up is to love. You dare to love—and hatred will come out of the cave and try to bash you. You dare to care—and someone will rise up to question your motives. You dare to tell the truth—and falsehood will come slithering out from under a rock and hiss its lies about you. You dare to do good—and evil will rise up against you and try to destroy you.

Why does that happen? Because people who never turn a hand to help others can't stand it when someone else does. Those good acts bring into question their own selfishness, and they will try to stamp out goodness in order to justify their own apathetic uncaring ways.

Fred Craddock tells about a young couple in a small town in the Midwest. They had a son who played on the high school football team. He didn't get to play much, but his parents were always there, dressed in the school colors, waving their banners, cheering for the team. One Friday night after the game, as they started home with their son, they passed a boy walking down the side of the road. He was the star of the team, a running back. He was just a tenth-grader, barely sixteen, but a natural athlete. He had scored three touchdowns that night.

They stopped and offered him a ride. He got in the car and they drove to his home, but the house was dark. They were concerned.

"Are your folks not home? Would you like us to wait with you till they get here?"

"O, no thanks."

"Were they at the game?"

"No." Then the story unfolded.

His parents had left several days ago. He didn't know where they were, or when they'd be back, or even if they were coming back. He was the star of the team—and his parents had never seen him play. They

86

didn't care. They gave him no love, no encouragement, no support.

This good family became concerned about the boy. They took him home with them for the night. The next day, they contacted the school and found that quite a number of students were in similar predicaments. It was just a small town, but some of the kids didn't have any love or help at home.

So in cooperation with the school and the church, this couple formed a support group to help these young people. They opened their home to them. On Monday nights, they tutored the kids, on Wednesday nights, they had Bible study and sharing, and on Friday nights after the football games, they had parties for these young people. It was great and it grew. This couple led it and they were very good at it. It was helpful. The school was happy. The church was happy. The young people were happy.

But there were some heavy faces hanging over coffee cups down at the local cafe.

"You know what that couple's doing, don't you?"

"No, what are they doing?"

"Well, you know when you get these kids together, bad things happen; I read about it in the magazines. Drugs, dirty movies, illicit behavior. Why, there's no telling what that couple's doing to those young people."

"Nobody's that good—to give all that time and open their home like that. There's something bad going on over there, if you ask me—and I'm not the only one talking about it, either."

Whisper, whisper, whisper—the word got around town. The gossip became so bad that the man lost his job. The couple was crushed, absolutely heartbroken. They had to leave town and start their lives over in another place. And it was all a lie! There was not one word of truth in it. They were trying to do something good—and evil rose up against them.

It happens that way sometimes. You can do something Christian, and it will prick the consciences of those who aren't doing anything good, and they will hurt you. They will try to crucify you. I know it to be true. I have seen it happen. But the good news is this: Ultimately, God and righteousness will win, and God will share the victory with us.

In the meantime, what can we do? Well, like those early Christians, we can stand tall for righteousness. Unflinchingly, unwaveringly, uncompromisingly, we can hold high the torch of justice and goodness—and trust God to bring it out right.

Believe in righteousness! Dedicate your life to goodness! Work night and day for love and justice—but understand that you may be persecuted and slandered. But do it anyway, and don't be afraid, because God is the Lord of life, and God will see you through.

And when you are persecuted, hold on to your commitment to God. Don't give up and don't sell out. Hold firmly to God. God will not fail you.

And hold on to the spirit of Christ. Don't descend to the level of your persecutors. Take the high road, come what may, and live in the spirit of Christ. Stand firm with him who, when he was reviled, reviled not again. Don't use their tactics. Don't get into their gutter. To quote a friend of mine, "Never wrestle with a pig in a pigpen. You'll just get dirty, and he likes it!"

Finally, hold on to your trust in God. Remember how Corrie Ten Boom, a prisoner of war in a World War II death camp, expressed her trust in God when she wrote *The Hiding Place:* "There is no pit so deep that God is not deeper still." That says it all—and that's what the eighth Beatitude is all about. Come what may, we can trust God!

II

Instructions for Moral Living

The Ten Commandments

1. You shall have no other gods before me.
2. You shall not make for yourself an idol.
3. You shall not make wrongful use of the name of the Lord your God.
4. Remember the sabbath day, and keep it holy.
5. Honor your father and your mother.
6. You shall not murder.
7. You shall not commit adultery.
8. You shall not steal.
9. You shall not bear false witness against your neighbor.
10. You shall not covet.

Exodus 20:1-17

9
Putting God First

Exodus 20:1-7
Commandment 1:
You shall have no other gods before me.
Commandment 2:
You shall not make for yourself an idol.
Commandment 3:
You shall not make wrongful use
of the name of the LORD your God.

• A missionary in a deep, dark corner of Africa was trying to convert a native chief. Now, the chief was very old, and the missionary was very Old Testament—that is, his version of Christianity leaned heavily on the "Thou shalt nots!"

The elderly native chief listened patiently and finally said, "I do not understand this religion of yours. You mean I cannot steal?"

"That's right!" said the missionary.

"You mean I can't take my neighbor's wife?"

"Quite right!"

"Or his ivory or his oxen?"

"Precisely!" answered the missionary.

"You mean I can't dance the war dance? I can't ambush the enemy? I can't kill?"

93

"Absolutely right," said the missionary.

Then the native chief said regretfully, "But I can't do any of those things anyway—I am too old!" Then, with a wave of the hand, the aged chief added, "To be old, and to be Christian—it is the same thing!"

• Some months ago, I pulled into a service station in southwest Houston to get some gas. I met a young man there who told me that he really enjoyed our televised church service. I invited him to come join us, but he said he was not ready to make that kind of commitment right now. He was still "enjoying life," having a great time sowing his wild oats. He indicated that maybe he would come and get involved in the church some day when he was older.

But then he added, "To tell you the truth, Jim, I'm really hoping for one of those neat death-bed conversions!"

Unfortunately, many people today share the confusion and misunderstanding of the Christian faith expressed by that old native chief in the deep dark corner of Africa, and that young man in the service station in southwest Houston. They think of God as one who frowns on our fun, slaps our hands, and says constantly, "Naughty, naughty, mustn't do!" They think of Christianity as something old, joyless, negative, prohibitive. For these people, religion does not give life; it takes life away.

This kind of negativism is a real misunderstanding of the Christian faith. We need always to remember that Christianity is good news! That's what the word *gospel* means—"good news; glad tidings." God is not only a comfort; God is a joy. God is the source of all pleasure. God is light and laughter. God is the Giver of Life—real life, abundant life, full life, eternal life. And our chief purpose in life is to worship, serve, and enjoy God forever.

Often this misunderstanding of Christianity as negative and prohibitive emerges from a false interpretation of the Ten Commandments. The truth is that many people wrongly regard the Commandments as a burdensome set of narrow, rigid thou-shalt-not prohibitions, instead of a positive call to a courageous and meaningful life of love and service to God and to other people.

We are to obey the Commandments strictly and fervently, but with a positive, joyous attitude, rather than a heavy, negative down-in-the mouth spirit. The fact is that we should be supremely grateful to God for the Ten Commandments. They tell us clearly how things are, how things work, how life holds together, how God meant things to be.

Anyone who is awake enough to "smell the coffee" can easily see that life is better when we love God and other people; life is better when we respect our parents and tell the truth; life is better when we are honest, faithful, kind, and gracious in all our relationships. That's the way God meant it to be, and life works better for us when we live daily by these dependable spiritual laws.

Think of it like this. Just as we know, without question, that there are certain scientific laws we can count on, and just as we know, without question, that if we break those scientific laws, we suffer the consequences, there are also dependable spiritual laws in our world. These dependable spiritual laws are spelled out for us in the Ten Commandments.

95

You see, we don't really break the Commandments. We talk about breaking them, but we can't really break them, because they are unbreakable. Whatever we do, they remain intact. We are the ones who are broken when we disobey them.

For example, if I climbed to the top of the church spire and jumped off, I would disobey the law of gravity, but I would be the one broken, not the law of gravity. It would still be there, just as strong and dependable as ever. I would not have broken the law; I simply would have proved it.

In like manner, if I choose to disobey the Ten Commandments, I'm the one who is broken. These are not the Ten *Suggestions*. They are our spiritual roots. They are the unshakable, unchanging spiritual laws of God, and they are just as dependable as the law of gravity. Frederick Buechner, in *Wishful Thinking*, puts it like this:

There are basically two kinds [of law]: (1) law as the way things ought to be, and (2) law as the way things are. An example of the first is NO TRESPASSING. An example of the second is the law of gravity.

God's law has traditionally been spelled out in terms of category No. 1, a compendium of do's and don'ts. These do's and don'ts are the work of moralists and when obeyed serve the useful purpose of keeping us from each other's throats. They can't make us human but they can help keep us honest.

God's law *in itself*, however, [actually] comes under category No. 2 and is the work of God. It has been stated in eight words: "He who does not love remains in death" (I John 3:14). Like it or not, that's how it is. If you don't believe it, you can always put it to the test just the way if you don't believe the law of gravity, you can always step out a tenth-story window. (pp. 50-51)

The Ten Commandments tell us how things are, how life works best, and they are as valid for us now as they were for Moses and the people of Israel—and indeed for all people who have lived or ever will live on the face of this earth. They are not a set of negative rules that Moses decided to draw up one day to keep the people in line. They are God's eternal principles, woven into the very fabric of life.

Even though all but one of the Commandments are expressed in the negative form, each one has implicit within it a positive affirmation of life—especially when interpreted in the spirit of Jesus Christ our Lord. Indeed, Jesus summed them all up in a positive note when he said, "You shall love the Lord your God with all your heart, soul, mind, and strength, and your neighbors as yourself."

Without question, the positive principles of the Ten Commandments underscore for us the unwavering foundational principles of morality and the spiritual life in this universe.

In *Foundation for Reconstruction,* Elton Trueblood turns the Commandments around, takes them out of the negative, and reveals their positive principles poetically:

> Above all else love God alone;
> Bow down to neither wood nor stone.
> God's name refuse to take in vain;
> The Sabbath rest with care maintain.

Respect your parents all your days;
Hold sacred human life always.
Be loyal to your chosen mate;
Steal nothing, neither small nor great.
Report, with truth, your neighbor's deed;
And rid your mind of selfish greed.

Thus, in the Ten Commandments, we see not a list of negative rules or taboos, but a positive, powerful, emphatic call for love for God and love for one another. Notice how they can be outlined in four groupings:

1. The first three Commandments call for love and devotion to God. (Put God first, worship only God, be faithful to God's name).

2. The fourth Commandment calls for love and devotion to the church. (Remember the holy day of the Lord).

3. The fifth and seventh Commandments call for love and devotion to the family. (Honor your parents and be faithful in marriage).

4. The sixth, eighth, ninth, and tenth Commandments call for love and devotion to other people. (Be honest, gracious, truthful, and kind with your neighbors). Look with me now at what it means to be loyal to God, as described in the first three Commandments.

"YOU SHALL HAVE NO OTHER GODS BEFORE ME."

Trueblood translated it like this: "Above all else love God alone." This simply means that God comes first. God is number one. God gets first place. God is the one

98

and only Lord of life. Put God first—this is what the first Commandment demands.

Now, the very fact that this command to put God first is the first of the Ten Commandments obviously underscores its importance. It means that we must give God our undivided allegiance, our highest loyalty. In the Sermon on the Mount, Jesus put it like this: "Strive for [God's] kingdom, and these things will be given to you as well" (Luke 12:31). In other words, Jesus simply meant, "Make God the King of your life!"

Have you seen the new generic greeting card? Birthday, anniversary, Halloween, Easter—it fits every occasion. On the outside, is printed: Generic Greeting Card. When you open it up, it says, WHATEVER! Many people go through life like that—just giving their allegiance to whatever the latest fad might happen to be. But this first Commandment grabs us by the scruff of the neck and says, "Wait a minute! That will not work. You can't chase every new wind that blows. God is the one and only Lord of life. Put God first! Give your allegiance to the one God!"

Joe Dumars is a professional basketball player for the Detroit Pistons. In 1989, he led the Pistons to the NBA title and was voted Most Valuable Player. The most impressive thing about Joe Dumars is his attitude, his great team spirit. In college, he was the leading scorer at McNeese State, but with Detroit, he unselfishly gives himself for the team, doing anything they need. He plays any role he is assigned—off guard, playmaker, shooting guard—and especially defends against the opponent's best player.

With great dedication, Joe does what is needed. Characteristic of his unselfishness, he gave his championship ring to his father. Joe Dumars practices professionally what Jesus did each day of his life. Jesus was ready to do God's will, no matter what—preacher, teacher, healer, victim—because he came not seeking his own will, but the will of God.

This is a hard lesson to learn in a society that stresses "doing your own thing." Sometimes I wonder to what extent today's worst ills—substance abuse, economic exploitation, environmental pollution—are a result of this "do your own thing" stance. Maybe we should stress "do God's thing." That's what this first Commandment is about: Above all else, love God alone. Put God first.

"YOU SHALL NOT MAKE FOR YOURSELF AN IDOL."

Trueblood puts it this way: "Bow down to neither wood nor stone."

A cartoon shows two sailors coming out of the base chapel one Sunday morning. The chaplain has just preached a sermon on the Ten Commandments.

One sailor, feeling guilty, says to the other, "Well, at least I never made a graven image!" He is implying that he has broken all of the other Commandments, but not this one. But he is wrong. The truth is that this is the one we break most often.

Idolatry—the worship of something other than God—is our most prolific sin. We may not fall down before golden calves or statues or stones, but there are plenty of false gods being worshiped these days. If we give our ultimate loyalty to things that have no lasting value, that is idolatry. If we long for money or pleasure or power or material possessions, that is idolatry. If we worship success or position or social standing, that too is a violation of the second Commandment, and these kinds of misplaced loyalties will come back to haunt us.

The decade of the 1980s has been called the decade of greed and materialism. As it gave way to the 1990s, the media presented story after story about the people and events of those "decadent years." One magazine devoted a special edition to an analysis of the decade. The headline read: "The 80s—Brash Was Beautiful, and the Only Sin Was Not to Win." It's true that decade is now behind us but it's also true that many people today continue to fall down and worship at the altar of greed.

But this second Commandment brings us up short: "Now, wait a minute. That will not work! You may spend a lot of time and effort with those false gods you make, but at some point, you are going to come face to face with the God who made you. First—No other Gods! Second—No worship of false gods!"

"YOU SHALL NOT MAKE WRONGFUL USE OF THE NAME OF THE LORD YOUR GOD."

This Commandment carries with it several meanings. For one thing, it means no profanity—don't use God's name in irreverent ways. I don't know about you, but I am sick of profanity. In movies, songs, plays—even on T-shirts and bumper stickers—everywhere we go, we are inundated with profanity, and our world excuses it by calling it, of all things, *adult* language. To me, it sounds so immature, so childish, so sinful.

Second, it means we must not use God's name to fortify a lie or to give weight to our own ideas. As Jesus put it, "Let your yes be yes and your no be no!" We must not swear by God's name.

But there is a third meaning here. We must not give God lip service that is not backed up by righteous living. Be earnest, genuine, sincere. Practice what we preach. Don't do anything that dishonors the name of God. As Christians, we take on the name of Christ. We belong to Christ. We represent Christ. We are "of Christ." That's what the word *Christian* means—"one who is of Christ." To not take that seriously, to not live daily in Christ's Spirit is to take God's name in vain. Keeping with the first two, this third Commandment also calls for love and devotion to God.

Angus, a church member in Scotland, told his pastor, with great enthusiasm, that he planned to go to the Holy Land.

"And when I get there," he said, "I will read the Ten Commandments aloud from the very top of Mount Sinai, and I know I'll be close to God."

"Angus," the minister replied, "if you really want to be close to God, take my advice. Just stay home and keep the Commandments. That's what God wants."

Indeed so! The calling of our Christian faith is to put God first in our day-to-day living. Life works best when we give God first place in our daily lives and love God with all our heart, soul, mind, and strength.

10
Letting Our Souls Catch Up with Our Bodies

Exodus 20:8-11
Commandment 4:
Remember the sabbath day, and keep it holy.

Remember the Sabbath day and keep it holy. Over the years, this Commandment has been greatly misunderstood, misinterpreted, and distorted in a number of ways. So let's begin by clearing out the underbrush, getting rid of those distortions.

This Commandment should not be understood in a narrow, restrictive way. The stress should not be on what *cannot* be done on the Lord's day, and yet that is precisely what many folks have done with this Commandment. They have made it heavy and sad and burdensome.

Shortly after the Commandment was given, strict legalists went to work to draw up some restrictive laws that so encumbered the Sabbath that it became a day of drudgery. By the time of Christ, there were 1,521 things you could not do on the Sabbath day. Many of these laws were ridiculous, and virtually all of them were negative, prohibitive, restrictive.

For example, you could not light a fire, cook a meal, look into a mirror, lift a child, pick up a needle, save a drowning man, or wear false teeth on the Sabbath. You could not take a bath, because the steam from the hot water might clean the floor, and this would be an act of labor and a violation of the fourth Commandment.

You could not shave or ride a horse or move a lamp or take medicine on the Sabbath day. If your ox fell into a ditch, you could pull it out, but if *you* fell into a ditch, you would have to stay there until the next day.

Eggs laid on the Sabbath day could not be eaten because the hens had been working. If a flea bit you on the Sabbath, you could not scratch it or hit it. You had to let the flea bite in peace, because to strike at it would be hunting, and that was strictly forbidden. Once when a fire broke out in Jerusalem on the Sabbath, afraid of violating the fourth Commandment, people let it burn and three persons died.

Well, as you can see, the scribes had gotten carried away, and things had gotten out of hand. In their passion for detail and definition, they had added more and more laws, which became more and more petty, ridiculous, and burdensome.

The gift of the Sabbath was the symbol of God's love for us. The Sabbath was meant to be a time of rest and celebration, a day of joy and thanksgiving, a time to *charge* our spiritual batteries, not drain them. This is what Jesus was showing us when he pointed out that the Sabbath is here to help us, not to hinder us; that the Sabbath is the milestone of the week, not the millstone.

But, unfortunately, over the years, some folks have brought this kind of heavy, burdensome, negative misunderstanding to the fourth Commandment. They want to emphasize with pious glee all the things we cannot do on the Sabbath day, and that is a gross distortion of what this Commandment is all about. The fourth Commandment, "Remember the Sabbath day, and keep it Holy," should not be understood in a narrow, restrictive way.

The Commandment should not be understood in a loose, permissive way. This is the flip side of the coin. The reverse of restrictive legalism is that anything goes— anything is permissive on the Sabbath.

In this view, Sunday is a holiday, but has long ago ceased to be a holy day. The people who take this stance will go everywhere but to church on Sunday. They do everything except worship, and they excuse themselves by saying things like, "Well, I was there in spirit," or, "I just wasn't in the mood today," or, "I can feel just as close to God at the lake."

One of the great writers of our time, C. S. Lewis, was married to another outstanding author, Joy Davidman. She once wrote a fascinating book on the Ten Commandments, titled *Smoke on the Mountain*.

In her chapter on this fourth Commandment, a creative piece of satire exposes the shallow ways some folks observe the Sabbath, when an imaginary student from Mars comes down to Earth to study Earth people and the ways we worship. Here is what the young Martian said about us:

> The creatures of the third planet are sun worshipers. One day in every seven is set apart for the adoration of their deity, weather permitting. Their rituals vary, and each apparently involves a special form of dress; but all are conducted in the open air, and most seem to require the collection of enormous crowds. Some creatures gather in vast arenas, to watch strangely garbed priests perform elaborate ceremonies involving a ball and variously shaped

instruments of wood. . . . Others, no doubt the mystics and solitaries of their religion, prefer to address the ball themselves with long clubs, singly or in groups of two or four, wandering in green fields. Some, stripping themselves almost naked in their ecstasy, go down to the seashore in great throngs and there perform their rites, often hurling themselves into the waves with frenzied cries. . . . After the ceremonial immersion, [they] anoint themselves with holy oils and stretch themselves out full length with eyes closed, in order to surrender themselves entirely to silent communion with the Sun Deity.

Human sacrifice, sad to say, is also practiced, the instrument of death being a four-wheeled metal car. . . .

There exists, however, a small sect of recalcitrants or heretics that does not practice sun worship. These may be identified by their habit of clothing themselves more soberly and completely than the sun worshipers. They too gather in groups, but only to hide from the sun in certain buildings of doubtful use, usually with windows of glass colored to keep out the light. It is not clear whether these creatures are simply unbelievers or whether they are excommunicated from sun worship for some offense.

Was the student from Mars wildly wrong, or was he painfully right? We might as well admit it—many people today observe Sunday as anything but a day of holiness.

Recently I heard a television interview with a top executive for one of the major corporations of America. Drugs have become such a problem for his company that they are now doing periodic drug testing of employees. And he said, "We always do them on Monday mornings." The implication is that Saturday and Sunday are the days when people are most likely to experiment with drugs.

This mistaken idea that anything goes on Sunday,

the shallow position that being in church is not really that important, the distorted notion that "I don't need to be in church on Sunday; I can worship God anywhere" is a gross misinterpretation of this fourth Commandment. The point is clear. This Commandment should not be taken either in a narrow, restrictive way or in a loose, permissive way.

The fourth Commandment should not be understood in a limited way. Some people misunderstand this Commandment in this disturbing way. They distort the Commandment without realizing it, unknowingly imprisoning and paralyzing themselves. They want to limit God to "Sunday only." They have the mistaken notion that Christianity is basically a one-day-a-week affair. They come to church on Sunday to appease God, and then ignore God the rest of the week. They feel that Sunday is for God, and Monday through Saturday are for them. This idea that the church has nothing to do with our daily lives and work-a-day world, that God can somehow be locked up in the church, is a gross distortion. It recognizes that God is Lord of the Sabbath, but forgets that God is Lord of Life.

You are probably familiar with that famous painting of Christ standing at the door and knocking. Christ wants to come through the door, but there is no door knob—so he knocks and waits, wanting us to open the door and let him in. Traditionally, we have interpreted the painting as if the door is the door to our hearts, and it can be opened only from the inside. Christ wants to come into our hearts, but he will not force his way in. We need to open the door to let him in.

That is a beautiful thought, and it probably is what the artist originally had in mind, but sometimes I find myself thinking that in the painting, Christ is *inside* the church. Perhaps he is knocking on the church door from the inside, wanting us to open it so he can go out into all the world.

We must not lock Christ up in the church. We must let him go out to a needy world, a world starved for him and his love, and for the salvation he brings. He is not only the Lord of the Sabbath. He is the Lord of Life and the Savior for all people.

If we should not take this fourth Commandment in a narrow, restrictive way, or in a loose, permissive way, or in a shallow, limited way, what then is the proper understanding of this Commandment? Let me suggest a few ideas, and I'm sure you will think of others.

SUNDAY IS A DAY OF REST

From the creation story in Genesis to the benediction in the Book of Revelations, the Bible makes it dramatically clear that there is a rhythm to life—a rhythm of work and worship, labor and rest. An old Greek Proverb puts it like this: "The bow that is always bent will finally cease to shoot at all."

O how we need to hear and heed this Commandment—those of us who live in this frantic, pressure-packed world, rushing at break-neck speed through life, burning the candle at both ends. We can relate to the man who went to his doctor, complaining of burnout. He was worn, weary, and frazzled. The doctor told him that he was foolishly overextending himself, that he would have to slow down.

Impatiently, the man replied, "Look, doctor, I didn't

come here to get a lecture about burning the candle at both ends. I came here for more wax!" But there is no more wax, not even a miracle drug. We must stop and rest. God made us that way. God knows how we are wired up; God did the wiring, and that's why God knows we need this Commandment.

In *Thunder on the Mountain*, Cecil Myers tells about a group of American explorers who went to Africa, where they hired natives to be their guides. The first day they rushed through the jungle. And on the second day they were up at dawn, ready to push forward. And likewise on the third, fourth, fifth, and sixth days.

On the seventh day, the American explorers were up early again, anxious to get started. But they noticed that their guides were lying very quietly in their places.

"Come on," shouted the Americans, "we are in a hurry!"

But the lead guide replied quietly in his broken English, "We no go today. We rest. Let souls catch up with bodies." Well, that's what we are to do on Sunday. We are to rest. We are to slow down. We are to center in on God. We are to let our souls catch up with our bodies. We are to recharge our spiritual batteries.

SUNDAY IS A DAY OF REMEMBERING

Sunday is a time to recall the great spiritual lessons of the past and to remember again, by the inspiration of the Holy Spirit, the real priorities of the present. One of my favorite quotes outside the Bible is something William Barclay said toward the end of his life: "I am an old man now, and over the years I have learned that there are very few things in life that really matter—but those few things matter intensely!" The church helps us to remember what those things are.

Love for God, love for people, love for family, honesty, integrity, justice, grace, forgiveness, kindness—those are the things that really matter. I don't know nearly as much about those good things as I would like to know, but what I do know about them, I found in the church.

That's why worship in church on Sunday is so important. It's the day we come together as a community of faith, hope, and love, to remember together—to remember the word of God, the will of God, the ways of God, the promises of God, the call of God, the saving grace of God. I don't know about you, but I need that community experience every week. I need that day of rest. I need that day of remembering.

SUNDAY IS A DAY OF RESURRECTION

The word *Sabbath* literally means "seventh," and of course the seventh day is Saturday. So why do Christians worship on Sunday? It is because, for Christians, every Sunday is a little Easter, a new beginning. Every Sunday, we celebrate the resurrection.

My friend Joe Zink had many wonderful qualities, but the thing I remember most about him was the radiance of his face on Sunday mornings. I don't think I have ever seen anyone who loved to be in church any more than Joe Zink. His face glowed with the joy of it. It was a day of new life and resurrection for him.

110

Several years ago, after a courageous battle with cancer, Joe died on a Sunday, right at the time of morning worship. At his funeral, I spoke of Joe's contagious smile and bright countenance on Sunday, and I mentioned that it seemed somehow fitting that Joe's "entrance into heaven" had come on a Sunday morning, because Sunday, for us Christians, is the day of resurrection.

The Lord's Day is a day of rest, a day of remembering, and a day of resurrection.

God gave us this Commandment because God knows how much we need it. Every now and then, we need to rest, we need to remember, and we need to be reborn.

11
It Takes More Than Four Walls to Make a Home

Exodus 20:12, 14
Commandment 5:
Honor your father and your mother.
Commandment 7:
You shall not commit adultery.

During World War II, a kindly older gentleman who lived in a hotel here in the United States became acquainted with a young preschool girl, the daughter of a serviceman. The man noticed the little girl playing daily in the hotel lobby. It was the only place she had to play, but she didn't seem to mind. In conversation with the little girl, he found out that because of the war, the serviceman and his family had moved time after time, from place to place, and now the hotel was their residence.

One day as they were talking together, the man said to the little girl, "What a pity that you and your family don't have a home."

The little girl answered with a deep wisdom, "Oh, we have a home. We just don't have a house to put it in!"

This story underscores a basic truth of life. It takes more than a house to make a home. It takes more than a father, a mother, and some children to make a real family. It takes love, patience, commitment, energy, communication, trust, faith—and a lot of hard work. Christian homes don't just happen. Christian families don't just pop up out of nowhere. They must be worked out, nurtured, developed, tended, cherished—and renewed each and every day.

The fifth and seventh Commandments recognize this, and they command love and loyalty to the family. O how we in this modern world need to hear afresh these Commandments! Family life is breaking down all around us, and it is tearing our society apart—drug problems, homelessness, sexual promiscuity, violence, public profanity, emotional illness, crime—these frightening social problems are strangling the very life out of our world. And most of them are significantly impacted by the breakdown of family life in our time. In any jail or prison today, you will discover that the problems of nine out of ten of the people being held there are rooted in a bad situation at home, a destructive family life.

Did you know that 85 percent of crime in the United States today is drug-related? And it is increasing every year! And, did you know that the primary cause of drug abuse is low self-esteem? This means that the drug problem is more a spiritual problem than a medical one. It means also that we need to cultivate in our children a healthy self-esteem and a firm spiritual strength. There is no question about it! Those most likely to experiment with drugs or get hooked on drugs are those who feel insecure; those who feel not quite able to face up to the stresses of life; those who feel that they can't have a good time, or face a problem, or make a decision on their own. Such people are so insecure that they think they have to have some help, some crutch, some drug.

Research has shown that the earlier prevention efforts begin in the home, the greater the likelihood of lasting success. So the point is clear. Parents must build their children's self-esteem; emphasize self-worth and self-respect; teach independent decision-making; remind them constantly that they are special—special to their parents and special to God.

Parents must introduce their children to Christ, live the Christian faith before them, keep them in church and Sunday school, teach them the Scriptures, teach them to pray. But even more important, parents should pray with their children and make them dramatically aware of how much they and God and the church love them. It's wonderful to provide children with a nice, comfortable home. It's important to meet all of their physical needs. But the truth is, that's not enough! More than anything, children need love.

Some years ago, a noted American psychoanalyst, Dr. Rene Spitz, made a documentary film about an orphanage in South America. The orphanage was well run. The physical needs of the children were well met. The workers were well trained and competent. But the home was greatly understaffed. There were 97 babies! The staff had time only to feed, clothe, and bathe the children. There was simply no time to hold them or play with them, no time to sing to them or talk to them. Their physical needs were routinely met—and then the children were left alone.

115

The isolation and loneliness proved to be destructive, even fatal. In the first year, 27 died; the second year, 7 more died. These tragic deaths took place even though all the physical needs of the children were being efficiently met. Those who did survive showed grave symptoms of abnormality and the inability to relate meaningfully to others. Twenty-one became hopeless neurotics. The lack of love was the culprit! We cannot live by bread alone. It is our love relationships that count most and make life worthwhile—and those relationships must start early at home.

Now, of course, healthy love for children does not mean letting them do anything they want. It does not mean letting them run wild. Children need parameters and guidelines. A few years ago, our city police department published a circular titled *For Parents: 12 Easy Ways to Turn Your Children into Delinquents*:

1. Begin at infancy to give your children everything they want. In this way, they will grow up to believe the world owes them a living.

2. When they pick up bad language, laugh at them. This will make them think they are cute.

3. Never give them any spiritual training. Wait until they are 21 and then let them decide for themselves.

4. Avoid the use of the word *wrong*. It may develop a guilt complex. This will condition them to believe later, when they are arrested for stealing a car, that society is against them and they are being persecuted.

5. Pick up everything they leave lying around— books, shoes, clothes. Do everything for them so they will be experienced in throwing all responsibilities onto others.

6. Let them read any printed matter they can get their hands on. Be careful that the silverware and

116

drinking glasses are sterilized, but let their minds feast on garbage.

7. Quarrel frequently in the presence of your children. In this way they will not be too shocked when the home is broken up later.

8. Give children all the spending money they want. Never let them earn their own way. Why should they have things as tough as you had them?

9. Satisfy their every craving for food, drink, and comfort. See that every sensual desire is gratified. Denial may lead to harmful frustration.

10. Always take their side against neighbors, teachers, police officers. They are prejudiced against your children.

11. When they get into trouble, apologize for yourself by saying, "I never could do anything with them."

12. Prepare for a life of grief. You will be likely to have it.

Those are tough words, but words we need to hear and think about.

Right here in the middle of the Ten Commandments are these two Commandments that underscore the tremendous importance of family life. The fifth and seventh Commandments call for love and loyalty to the family. Let's think about them one at a time.

"HONOR YOUR FATHER AND YOUR MOTHER."

In a shopping mall once, I heard a young teenager call his mother a "dumb, stupid nitwit." It sounded so obscene, so profane. How do you feel when you hear someone say something like, "My old lady is so uptight," or "I'll put the bite on the old man for a couple of bucks." I don't know about you, but it bothers me to hear people talk to, or about, their parents like that. I'm sure it must bother God, too, because God put this Commandment about honoring our parents right in the heart of the Ten Commandments.

The first four Commandments deal with our relationship with God; the last six deal with interpersonal relationships. It's no accident that the fifth Commandment has to do with loyalty to the family, because unless we learn to live together in the family, we aren't likely to learn how to get along with anybody anywhere. This fifth Commandment, to honor your father and your mother, carries with it three different meanings.

First, it has to do with giving honor and respect to our ancestors, the mothers and fathers of the past who were the pioneers of our faith, the trailblazers for Christianity.

How can we walk into the church without thinking about those great people who went before us and started this church in such a magnificent way? For years, committed people worked and sacrificed to give us what we have today. We must not take that lightly.

How can we read the Bible and study church history without thinking of the two thousand years of Christianity in which devoted Christian people labored, in spite of dungeon, fire, and sword, to bring us this incredible heritage? We must not take that for granted. We must give honor to those mothers and fathers of the past.

Second, this fifth Commandment tells us to give honor to our parents of the present. Kabod, the Hebrew word here

118

translated as "honor," is a broad and deep term, meaning to respect, to cherish, to accept, to obey, to take seriously, to treat with courtesy, to listen to, to give weight and authority to, to love. In a phrase, it means to value highly. Do you honor your parents like that? That's what God commands.

The third meaning of this fifth Commandment is that parents should be honorable. I heard a story about a little girl who came one day to her mother with the age-old question, "Mother, what is God like?" The mother hesitated in the presence of so great a question and finally said, "Dear, go ask your daddy." So the little girl went to her father with her search for God. But he too hesitated. Neither parent could answer her question. That story reminded me of a bit of free verse I once read:

> I asked my mother what God was like,
> She did not know.
> Then I asked my father.
> He did not know.
>
> I think if I had lived as long as my
>   mother and my father have,
> I would know something about God!

Think about that. Children should be able, when they look at their parents, to see that they know something about God. Children should see God in their parents; they should know that their parents are honorable.

It's interesting to note that this is the only Commandment that carries with it a promise. Honor your parents and your days will be long. At first glance, it sounds as if God is striking a bargain with us—"You be good to your parents, and I'll be good to you."

But actually, God is simply stating a fact of life: When parents are honored, when family life is strong, society endures. But when family life breaks down, it devastates society, because the home is the basic and most important unit in society. Education begins at home. Self-awareness begins at home. Respect for law and order begins at home. Concern for others, love for God, the church, the Scriptures, prayer—all these should begin at home.

That's what this fifth Commandment is about. A people with strong, stable homes, with close-knit families, with family love and loyalty—will have a long life in the land God gave them. A people that destroys the family will destroy itself. As the family goes, so go the people. "Honor your father and your mother, so that your days may be long."

"YOU SHALL NOT COMMIT ADULTERY."

What does this mean? Simply this—husbands and wives are to be faithful to their chosen mates! To show the danger of violating this commandment, I could tell about the book and movie *Fatal Attraction*, or I could point out the awful threat of the so-called social diseases, or I could simply mention the name of a certain athlete, or a certain politician, or a number of famous biblical characters—all of whom were brought down by their infidelities. But, let me deal with this in a more positive way.

Years ago, the famous explorers Lewis and Clark set out into the western wilderness to blaze a trail across the Rockies. They took with them a French guide who brought along his Native American wife. Life was rough and harsh for those men in the untamed wilderness.

Each night, the French guide would offer his wife to the men for a price. Each night, Lewis and Clark refused. Finally they crossed the last river east of the mountains and needed fresh horses and supplies. They asked the chief of a nearby Native American tribe for help.

In broken English, the chief replied, "No help white man. White man lie and cheat."

But then the wife of the French guide stepped out of the party and said to the chief, "These men are different! They keep their promises to their wives back home." Then she told the story of nights by the campfire and the refusal of these men to do wrong. She was able to persuade the chief, and he loaned Lewis and Clark the needed horses and supplies.

Then Lewis and Clark crossed the Great Divide, put their boats in the headwaters of the Columbia River, traveled to the Pacific, and claimed the great northwest. Their greatest achievement was based on their morality.

The first three Commandments call for love and loyalty to God. The fourth Commandment calls for love and loyalty to the church. The fifth and seventh Commandments call for love and loyalty to the family.

12
The Power of Respect and Goodwill

Exodus 20:15-17
Commandment 6:
You shall not murder.
Commandment 8:
You shall not steal.
Commandment 9:
You shall not bear false
witness against your neighbor.
Commandment 10:
You shall not covet.

Not long ago our daughter, Jodi, became extremely ill. When she went to see the doctor on a Monday morning, she was nauseated, dehydrated, and bent double with abdominal pain. The doctor took one look at her and put her in the hospital. All day Monday and Tuesday they ran tests, but they could not pinpoint the problem. Meanwhile, Jodi was hurting more and more, becoming weaker and weaker.

Finally, on Tuesday night she was rushed to the operating room, where emergency exploratory surgery was performed. Unbelievably, they discovered that Jodi's appendix had ruptured more than a month before! And somehow the poison had encapsulated itself, producing a large abscess.

The surgeons did an excellent job, and even though Jodi was critically ill, over time she has made a complete recovery. The stark fact is, however, that we almost lost her.

Although the events of that experience were horrendous and frightening, I must tell you that I saw a number of things in the experience that inspired me greatly. I was inspired by the power of prayer and the amazing courage and serenity that can come from a sense of God's presence with us.

I was inspired by the talent and commitment of good doctors, and by the tireless efforts of dedicated nurses as they perform their often thankless tasks. I was inspired by the miracle of healing, by the support and concern of caring friends, and by the incredible strength of a mother when her child is sick. And I was inspired by the love and candid expressions of children. Jodi is a schoolteacher, and her students in fourth grade wrote her some love letters that are classics. Let me share some of them with you. The first one is in poetic form.

Dear Mrs. DeHondt,
I'm hoping you get better
Because of this letter;
We just love you so much
Because of your special touch;
What I mean with this tune
Is Get Well Soon.

124

Another wrote:

> *Dear Mrs. DeHondt,*
> *I love you and I miss you very much.*
> *If a lady with brown hair and brown eyes*
> *comes by to see you and says "Hi,"*
> *that's my mom. I sent her.*

One nine-year-old girl had this to say . . .

Dear Mrs. D.,

> *Heard what happened to you and I think*
> *it is very totally gross. I am very*
> *sorry. Hope you get well soon enough to*
> *come see our Christmas play. I'm in it*
> *and I am very funny. It will make you*
> *feel better.*

A ten-year-old boy who was in Jodi's class last year wrote this:

> *Heard you were in the hospital. Not very*
> *fun, huh? Well, 5th grade is not real*
> *fun either. I hope you get out soon*
> *because your class is probably going*
> *wild. I know what you are going through*
> *is tough, but you can't be having a*
> *worse time than me because I'm fixing to*
> *take a test. Well, I love you and hope*
> *you get better.*

This last letter came from a nine-year-old boy whom some had once considered a "problem" child:

125

Dear Mrs. DeHondt:
I miss you. We need you back soon.
I've been praying for you.
Please get well soon.
You help me when I need help. You're the
best teacher I ever had. Here's a poem
for you. . .
Roses are red, violets are blue
I know a great teacher,
And that is you.

At the bottom of the page, he had drawn a picture of himself saying, "I miss you."

All those things touched me, but I saw something in Jodi's response to that frightening ordeal that inspired me most of all—her gracious spirit. Though she was very sick, heavily sedated, and in great pain, experiencing all kinds of discomfort, Jodi never failed to say "Thank you" to every single person who came into that hospital room.

They stuck her with needles continually, drew her blood repeatedly, gave her orders constantly, they pushed and poked her stomach incessantly, they attached tubes to her everywhere, they invaded her privacy—and to every person, she would say, "Thank you." To surgeons, specialists, therapists, nurses, aides, and housekeepers; to her husband, Danny, her friends, her in-laws, even to her mom and dad and her brother, Jeff—no matter what we did for her or to her, she would say, "Thank you."

It was a little thing and yet so big, because that expression of love and respect to everyone who happens by is a symbol of Jodi's Christian faith, not just something she learned from childhood as a rule of courtesy. Much more than that, it is a practical expression of her Christian faith. She really believes that the best way to show our love for God is to love God's children—all of them. She really believes that we can be the instruments of God's love, that God's love can flow through us and out to others. She really believes that our calling as Christians is to love God and to love other people.

And when you stop and think about it, that's what the Ten Commandments are all about. Here we discover a positive, emphatic, divine call for love and loyalty to God, and for love and loyalty to one another. Commandments 6, 8, 9, and 10 specifically call for love and devotion to other people. We are to respect their lives, their property, their names and reputations, and their good fortune. Let's take a closer look at these four Commandments.

"YOU SHALL NOT MURDER."

Positively speaking, this means that human life is sacred, sacred because it is beloved of God. This Commandment was designed to protect the most precious possession we have—life!

Up near the Lake of the Ozarks, a reptile farm has an unusual exhibit. A long series of glass cages house some of the most dangerous or poisonous snakes and lizards from all over the world. Tourists pass along, looking at one after another of these deadly creatures, until they come to the final cage, which has a big sign with these words: "The Most Dangerous Animal in the

World." Many people are surprised to see that the only thing in the cage is a mirror. You look in—and see your own face!

The message is clear. Of all the creatures on the face of the earth, humans are the most deadly, the most dangerous; humanity can do the most damage. But human beings can also do the most good—and that's what this sixth Commandment is about. When we read this commandment, "You shall not murder," in light of the New Testament, we understand that the spirit of this law means more than just abstaining from murder and hostility; it means promoting love and reconciliation.

Look what Jesus did with this Commandment. He extended it: "You have heard it was said . . . 'You shall not murder'. . . . But I say to you that if you are angry with a brother or sister, you will be liable to judgment." Jesus calls on us to stop murder at its very source—anger, hatred, vengeance. Jesus knew that hate is a real enemy to be overcome. Hate blinds, distorts, and it actually kills long before the deadly blow falls.

Undoubtedly, Cain had killed Abel a hundred times in his mind before he actually slew him in the field. Human life is sacred to God, and hatred is God's enemy. Hatred has no place in the heart of Christians.

I once heard about a man who set up Donatello's statue of a boy. He wanted to put light on the statue for effect, so he placed some lights on the floor. But with the lights shining from below, the boy's face looked horrid, grotesque, evil. The man tried every possible arrangement, to no avail. Then finally, he put the lights *over* the statue and let them shine down from above.

128

The man stood back and looked, and he was amazed—the lights shining from above made the boy look beautiful, attractive, valuable—like an angel!

What a parable! When we look at other people in the light of earth, they may look grotesque, and we may think, "Well, what difference does it make how I treat them?" But when we look at other people in the light of God's love, they look like angels, and we begin to see them as persons for whom Christ died.

What does this Commandment, "You shall not murder," mean for us today? It means that we should always hold human life as sacred. It means we should love, respect, and value the lives of other people, for they too are God's children; it means we should be loyal to others.

"YOU SHALL NOT STEAL."

Positively speaking, this means that we should steal nothing, neither small nor great. We should respect the rights and properties of others.

This Commandment must have been a great shock to the early Israelites! They had been nomads, and among nomads, stealing, pilfering, and looting from other tribes was both an accepted practice and a fine art. But you see, God knew that the sin of stealing is that the stealer gets his or her priorities all mixed up. A thief forgets what is really important in life. To steal is to say in effect, "To me, things are more important than people." To steal is to say, "I'm more important than you." Stealing violates the rights of others and the will of God.

We need to always remember that people are to be loved, not used, and that things are to be used, not loved. This eighth Commandment is tremendously relevant for us today because we live in a thing-centered world. Modern advertising, with all its enticements, can create a strong desire for more and more things. And this desire can make us do strange things.

All of us are like the little boy standing by the apple barrel in the country store. He kept looking at the apples, then looking away.

Finally the grocer went over and said, "Son, are you trying to steal an apple?"

"No sir," replied the little boy. "I'm trying real hard not to!"

Then there are some of us who cannot see our own dishonesty. One day a wife said to her husband, "You won't believe this, but our weekend guests stole four of our best towels."

"Well," answered the husband, "some people are like that, can't trust 'em, just made that way. By the way, which ones did they get?"

The wife said, "Those fluffy white ones with Hyatt Regency written on them!"

This eighth Commandment calls us to be honest in all our dealings! Respect the rights and properties of others! Don't steal anything! Be loyal to others!

"YOU SHALL NOT BEAR FALSE WITNESS."

Positively speaking, this means, "Be truthful! Report with truth your neighbor's deed." Do not gossip. Do not condemn. Do not deal in half-truths. Do not lie. Jesus warns us about this, and the apostle Paul lists sins of the "tongue" as one of the worst sins.

We have always heard that sticks and stones may break my bones, But words will never hurt me. There is only one thing wrong with that rhyme—it's just not true. Words do hurt. Some of our worst hurts come from words. It can make all the difference if we will hold our judgment of an event or a person until we have all the facts, the whole truth. All too often a hasty, faulty judgment, made on rumor or hearsay and passed cruelly on, has caused needless suspicion, suffering, heartache—even tragedy.

This prayer of Allen Stockdale could be prayed by each of us daily:

Dear Lord, look into my mouth and see what a cruel thing my tongue is. It seeks to ruin good reputations; it lies when crowded into a corner; it boasts to satisfy vanity, it runs on and on when silence would be golden; it does not report matters correctly; it has made trouble for me and my relatives, friends, and co-workers. Dear Lord, if you can adjust my tongue to truth and gentleness, love, and fairness, you will perform a miracle of compassion in the area where I live, move, and have my being.

This ninth Commandment means be truthful. But more than that, be kind, honest, and fair. Be gracious. Speak the truth in love. Be loyal to others. Or as they say in New England, "If it doesn't improve on the silence, just don't say it."

"YOU SHALL NOT COVET."

Positively speaking, this means to get rid of selfish greed. It means don't be envious, don't be jealous, don't be resentful of the good fortune of others.

The word *covet* means to desire, to crave, to long for or lust after something that belongs to another person. The Greek word for *covet* means "to grab, to grasp, to always want more." It refers to selfish greed—the kind that can't stand the thought of anyone else doing well. The covetous person wants all the gravy and all the glory.

In the parable of the prodigal son, the sin of the elder brother is covetousness. His brother has returned home safe and sound. The father is overjoyed to have the prodigal safely back in the family circle. He calls for a great Welcome Home party. The elder brother can't stand it. He is jealous, resentful. He disowns his brother and questions his father—and he misses the party.

That's what covetousness does to us. It cuts us off from people, and it cuts us off from God. In that story, the father is gracious, the elder brother is greedy; the father forgives, the elder brother fumes; the father rejoices, the elder brother resents. The point of the prodigal son parable is clear—God is loving toward us and wants us to act in loving ways. God is loyal to us and God wants us to be loyal to God and to one another.

Loyalty to God and loyalty to others. That's what the Ten Commandments are all about.

III

The
Bottom-line
Instruction

Jesus' New
Commandment

I give you a new commandment, that you love one another. Just as I have loved you, you also should love one another. By this everyone will know that you are my disciples, if you have love for one another.

John 13:34-35

13
And Along Came Jesus

John 13:34-35

I give you a new commandment, that you love one another. Just as I have loved you, you also should love one another. By this everyone will know that you are my disciples, if you have love for one another.

I recently had a moving religious experience—I rode in a taxi cab in New York City! Now, that will straighten out your priorities in a hurry! That religious experience was twofold in nature.

First, there was the element of stark fear. My life passed before my eyes as I wondered if I would make it to my destination alive and well. That thought was made all the more haunting when I realized during this taxi-cab thrill ride that, under my breath, I was nervously whistling the hymn "Nearer My God to Thee."

In addition, I noticed an interesting picture stuck on the back of the driver's seat—a picture of three men sitting at a table, with a microphone in front of each of them. All three were dressed to look like Jesus, but they represented three very different images. One was rather wild-eyed, bizarre looking, like a wild man of the

135

desert, a tough prophet of old. The second was macho looking—handsome, athletic, tanned, muscular, strong—a man's man. The third was a small, frail man, an obvious representation of the gentle Jesus, meek and mild. Under the picture was the caption, "Will the Real Jesus Please Stand Up?"

And that is precisely what is happening in John 13. The real Jesus is standing up and telling his disciples, and us, what he is all about and what he wants us to be about. And the word is love! The last will and testament of our Lord is love!

It's interesting to note that the Gospel of John is divided neatly into two parts. The first part (chapters 1 through 12) is written to show with dramatic signs and wonders that Jesus is, without question, the Son of God and the Savior of the world. Then with chapter 13, the second part begins. It describes the poignant march of Jesus to and through the cross, the last supper, the arrest, the trial, the crucifixion, and the resurrection.

In John 13, Jesus is in the upper room with his disciples. He knows the cross is near at hand, and he is giving his final instructions to his followers. He is thinking deep thoughts. He knows the time is short. Judas has just gone out to betray him. There is so much to tell them, but so little time, so here in this scene, he sums it all up in one statement: "I give you a new commandment, that you love one another . . . as I have loved you . . . . By this everyone will know that you are my disciples, if you have love for one another." In this powerful scene, the real Jesus stands up and tells us what he wants us to do.

Recently, as I was studying this powerful passage, I

was caught up in the drama of what Jesus is doing here with his disciples. He is trying to prepare his friends to go on without him, to take up the torch of his ministry. Suddenly my mind flashed back to a personal experience that occurred in May of 1950. It was a Thursday night shortly after my twelfth birthday. My father took my fourteen-year-old brother and me aside for a man-to-man talk. It was late at night, and my dad seemed unusually tired and drained.

He seemed very philosophical, and as I think back on it now, very intense. He leaned back in his chair, looked us straight in the eye and he began to talk.

"Now, I want you boys to grow up," he said. "You need to help out a little more around here and be more responsible. You need to learn how to take charge. You need to see what has to be done and do it without my having to tell you. I want you to be more thoughtful of your mother and your little sister. I want you to be kind and loving and mature."

He paused for a long time, looking at the floor, and then added something somewhat strange. "Life is uncertain," he said. "We just don't know how long I'll be here, and if something happens to me, you boys will have to grow up in a hurry and help your mother."

And three nights later, my father was gone. He died in a car wreck as he was being rushed to the hospital with a ruptured appendix. When my brother and I reported this conversation to the family, many of them said that he must have had a premonition, and he was getting us ready, setting the house in order. I think it's more likely that something connected with that bad appendix was bothering him. He was having strange sensations he didn't quite understand, but he knew that something was wrong. He was alarmed, and he was trying to prepare us for whatever might happen.

Something like that is what Jesus was doing with his disciples in John 13. He knew that his days with his disciples were numbered, and he was trying to get them ready. That's why this passage is so important. It's like saying to a preacher, "If you had one sermon to preach, what would it be?" Or saying to a professor, "If you had one great truth to convey to your students, what would you teach them?" Or to a parent, "If you had one message—only one—to leave with your children, what would you say to them?"

That's the tone, the impact, the significance of this passage in John 13. And in that powerful moment, Jesus gave them his best shot. He summed up his life, and our responsibility as His disciples, in that one statement.

There are many mountain-top moments in the Bible, and in my opinion, this is one of the highest peaks. If I were asked to select five Scripture passages that every Christian should memorize and write indelibly on their hearts, this statement would, without question, be one of them. We can better understand this powerful passage if we break it down into three parts:

• The new Commandment which Christ brought is the law of love.
• This love should be Christlike love.
• This Christlike love is the real sign of discipleship.

Let's look now at the specific parts of this amazing, unforgettable text.

"I GIVE YOU A NEW COMMANDMENT, THAT YOU LOVE ONE ANOTHER"

In this opening phrase, we discover the freshness of Christ, the uniqueness of Christ, the crux of Christ's life and teachings, the new message which Jesus Christ came to bring to our world—the message of Love!

Many years before Christ came, *the law of the land was revenge*—survival of the fittest, the law of the jungle: "If you do something bad to me, you had better watch out, because I'm going to get you back and then some! I will nurse my grudge to keep it warm and look eagerly for the occasion to get you back with fury and vengeance. You will pay dearly for what you did to me!" Revenge was the accepted and endorsed law of the land.

But then along came Moses, and he took the people a giant step forward—to *the law of retribution*. From revenge—"I'll get you back and then some," to retribution—"I'll get even," an eye-for-an-eye, a tooth-for-a-tooth. In other words, Moses said, "Now wait a minute. You can't get 'em back and then some. Revenge is wrong. You can do to them only what they did to you! No more! If someone breaks the little finger of your left hand, you can do only that much to that person. You can break the little finger of the left hand, but that's all. No more than that! That's all you can do!"

Since we live on this side of the cross, we sometimes look back at that eye-for-an-eye, tooth-for-a-tooth law of retribution and think it sounds primitive and harsh. But actually, at the time of Moses, it represented a huge step, a giant step toward a more civilized world. Moses was saying that revenge is wrong. Do no more to them than they did to you. Don't live any more by the cruel law of vengeance. Live instead by the law of retribution.

But then along came Jesus! And he introduced a new Commandment, a new way, a new approach, a radically new response—the law of Love! He told us that you don't have to get 'em back! You don't have to get even! You can forgive! You can love! If you want to know what is special about the teaching of Jesus, this is it: the new Commandment to love one another. Not revenge, not retribution, but love! That's what it's all about, and that's what Jesus was trying to communicate to his disciples in the upper room on the eve of his arrest. And that is the message he wants to give us. It's O.K. to Love! Indeed, it's beautiful! Nothing is more Godlike than love! You don't have to get 'em back. You don't have to get even. Love is the way! Love is the answer! "I give you a new commandment, that you love one another."

"JUST AS I HAVE LOVED YOU, YOU ALSO SHOULD LOVE ONE ANOTHER."

Now that's a powerful thought, isn't it? We are supposed to love as Christ loved—sacrificially, unselfishly, unconditionally. That kind of love is the only thing that can save this world—the sacrificial love of God in Christ Jesus—and we are called to live in that spirit.

Let me share with you the story of one high-school senior, and what his eight friends did for him to show their support and love when it was discovered that he had cancer. The prognosis for him is good, and the doctors are optimistic, but to fight the malignancy, he had to have chemotherapy. One of the things that bothered him most was the temporary hair loss caused by the chemotherapy. The thought of having to go back to school with no hair was painful.

But his friends devised a plan to help him. To ease his pain and embarrassment, to show their support and love as a gesture of empathy and authentic friendship, his friends did a remarkable thing—they all shaved their heads so he would not feel so alone and conspicuous when he returned to school! The front-page picture in the local newspaper showed them standing there in a semicircle, with Lance O'Pry in the middle, all with their heads shaved. And the headline read: "Everything We Do, We Do Together!"

The school principal said, "This is a unique bunch of fellows who are extremely close and extremely supportive of each other. I think it was super [the way] they banded behind him at such a critical time of his life."

One of the friends said, "We never would have done this as a prank. We did it because it had meaning. We were happy to do it."

We were happy to do it—what a touching, heartwarming story of genuine friendship! Somewhere in heaven, God is smiling. That kind of thoughtful gesture and sacrificial love is what Jesus came to show us and teach us.

That is the good news of our Christian faith. Jesus Christ is the hope of the world. His sacrificial love is the strongest, most powerful force this world has ever known. And if we want to serve him well, if we want to do good, if we want to be his disciples, if we want to hold high what he stands for, we will take up the torch of sacrificial love and live in that spirit.

"BY THIS EVERYONE WILL KNOW THAT YOU ARE MY DISCIPLES"

It is told that some years ago, General Omar Bradley boarded a commercial plane for a long trip. He was wearing a business suit, rather than his usual military attire. He found his assigned seat and began working on some important papers. Ironically, his seat-mate turned out to be a private in the U.S. Army, who was rather gregarious.

The private, who didn't recognize General Bradley, said to him, "Sir, we are going to be traveling together for some time, so I think it would be nice if we got to know each other. I'm guessing that you are a banker."

Bradley, not wanting to be rude, but wanting to get some work done, replied, "No, I am not a banker. I am General Bradley, a five-star general in the United States Army. I am head of the Joint Chiefs of Staff at the Pentagon in Washington, D.C."

After a slight pause, the young soldier said, "Well, sir, that is a very important job. I sure hope you don't blow it!"

Well, *we* have an important job too. We are to be the continuators of Christ's ministry of love. Let's not blow it! Let's never forget that love is the real sign of discipleship. It's good to be able to quote Scripture. It's good to be able to pray beautiful prayers. It's good to study theology. It's good to attend church regularly. But only when people see our love, only then do they really begin to see our faith.

Love is the real sign of discipleship. If we don't understand that, we blow it! Those were our Lord's last words to us: "I give you a new commandment, that you love one another." That's the bottom line!

Study Guide

R. Lee McKinzie

Introduction

1. Four C's serve as an outline of the Bible: Creation, Covenant, Christ, and Church. What relevance does each of these recurring themes of the Bible have today? What other recurring themes of the Bible are important to us as Christians?
2. Where do you turn first when you need help with a problem or question in your daily life? What role has the Bible played in providing guidance and instruction in your life? Are there sections or passages of the Bible that you turn to regularly, or that have been particularly helpful?
3. How have the Beatitudes, the Ten Commandments, and Christ's New Commandment influenced the way you live?

Chapter 1: It's Hard to Be Humble

1. How would you define the word *blessed*? How is

your definition different from or similar to the definition "near to the heart of God"?

2. How would you define "poor in spirit"? How does
the expression "humble-minded people" change
your understanding of this first Beatitude? What
does it mean to be humble?

3. We see in this chapter that humble-minded people
share at least three qualities: they trust God completely, treat others respectfully, and appreciate each
day. Do you know anyone who fits this description?
Describe that person. What other qualities do you
think a humble-minded person possesses?

4. What changes do you need to make in your life in
order to become more humble-minded?

Chapter 2: Near to the Heart of God

1. At what times in your life have you felt closest to
God? Has a time of grief ever brought you closer to
the heart of God? How would you describe God's
presence in your life at that time?

2. Defining mourning as "caring deeply" broadens our
understanding of the word. Even those of us who
never have lost a loved one have experienced sorrow for our sins and have been saddened by the
troubles and hurts of others. How has mourning in
these ways brought you closer to the heart of God?

3. Are we sometimes guilty of looking at the world
with dry eyes? In what ways do we need to be more
mournful today?

4. How has God comforted you at those times when
you have grieved or been hurt deeply? In what ways
has God given you "new strength"?

Chapter 3: Here Am I, Lord, Use Me!

1. Moses was one of the strongest and most courageous characters in the Bible, yet the Bible refers to
him as meek (Numbers 12:3 KJV). How does our
understanding of the word *meek* differ today from
the biblical understanding of the word? Using the
biblical definition, what other persons from the
Bible, from history, and from our own time would
you describe as meek? In what ways have these
individuals demonstrated their availability to
God—their willingness to serve and trust God?
2. What does it mean to be obedient to God? When
have you put God's will above your own? What
happened?
3. What does it mean to be "steadied by God's presence"? When has God given you just the strength
you needed in a given situation?
4. What does it mean to be a servant of God? Name
people from the Bible and from your own life who
are examples of self-giving servants. In what ways
have these persons made themselves available to
God?

Chapter 4: Thirsting for Goodness

1. Are you growing in morality, character, ethics, and
cleanliness in your personal life? Compare where
you were in your Christian commitment to "personal goodness" five years ago to where you are today.
Where would you like to be next year? Five years
from now? What specific steps can you take to get
there? What help do you need from others?
2. Do you agree that part of our calling as the church is

146

to be the "conscience of society"? Why, or why not?

3. In what ways is your church currently involved in social justice—in your community, your state, our nation, and our world? What unmet needs might you help to meet?

4. In what ways do you express your love for God? How do your relationships with others affect your relationship with God?

5. Can a person who is strong in personal goodness but weak in social justice or right relationships be called righteous? In other words, are all three qualities required for righteousness? Why, or why not? Give examples to support your answer.

Chapter 5: Mercy, the Virtue That Shines

1. What do you think it means to show mercy? Give an example from your life or the life of someone you know.

2. How has empathy with someone helped you to be forgiving or merciful?

3. How is looking at others in the spirit of Christ an act of generosity? How can this lead to mercy? Can you think of an example?

4. How is forgiveness related to mercy? do you believe it is possible to receive God's mercy without passing it on to others?

5. Is there someone to whom you need to show mercy? In what ways?

Chapter 6: The Dangers of Mask-wearing

1. When we truly value others, we automatically show our appreciation in loving ways. In what ways do

you "honor" the members of your family? In what ways do they "honor" you?

2. What does it mean to reach out in love to other people and reach up in love to God? Is it possible to do one without the other? Why?

3. What does being sincere have to do with being pure in heart?

4. In what ways are the pure in heart like children? How can we become more childlike?

5. How does having a right relationship with God and Jesus Christ change our hearts and eyes? What does it mean to see God everywhere?

Chapter 7: The Best Thing We Can Do for God

1. How does being a peacemaker reflect spiritual maturity?

2. How does patience lead to peacemaking? Give an example.

3. What do you think would happen if you treated everyone in your life with love and respect? How does living by the Golden Rule make us instruments of God's peace?

4. Are there situations in your life in which you might be more "tuned in" to Christ—more Christlike? How could you be a peacemaker in these situations?

Chapter 8: Come What May, We Can Trust God

1. What are the three forms of persecution suffered by the early Christians? Do we face these forms of persecution today? In what ways? What other kinds of persecution do we face as followers of Christ?

2. Personal persecution is perhaps the most common

form of persecution experienced by Christians today. How have you (or someone you know) experienced personal persecution as a Christian? What happened?

3. What are we to do when faced with persecution for our Christian beliefs or practices?

4. Have you ever been in a situation when you held firm to your Christian faith, despite pressure or persecution? What enabled you to trust in God completely? Why do you think some people are able to stand tall for righteousness in any situation, while others crumble under even the threat of trouble?

Chapter 9: Putting God First

1. If you had to explain what the Ten Commandments are to a non-Christian, what would you say? How would you describe their purpose? How would you prevent the person from developing a negative understanding of the Christian faith?

2. How would you contrast "doing your own thing" with "doing God's thing"? What does it mean to put God first in your life?

3. What are some of the "false gods" people worship today? Can a person desire material possessions or success or power or position or social standing without committing idolatry? Why, or why not?

4. Most often, we interpret the third Commandment as meaning that we should not use profanity or swear by God's name. In what other ways do we "take God's name in vain"—or dishonor the name of God?

5. What is the calling of our Christian faith? How can we show others that we love God with all our heart, mind, soul, and strength?

149

Chapter 10: Letting Our Souls
Catch Up with Our Bodies

1. We see in this chapter that there are three common misunderstandings of the fourth Commandment and of the purpose of the Sabbath, Sunday. Try to think of persons you know who demonstrate each understanding. What do you think has contributed to their attitude about Sunday? In what ways may you be guilty of wrong attitudes about Sunday?
2. Sunday is a day of rest. The African natives knew a wise truth: We need to let our souls catch up with our bodies. What does this mean to you? How does attending church on Sunday help your soul to catch up with your body? What other things can you do to recharge your spiritual batteries?
3. Sunday is a day of remembering. What important things does attending church on Sunday help you to remember? What else helps you to remember things that, as William Barclay said, "matter intensely"?
4. Sunday is a day of resurrection. In what way are we to be "reborn" each Sunday? What do you think prevents many Christians from experiencing Sunday as a day of resurrection?

Chapter 11: It Takes More Than Four Walls
to Make a Home

1. In what ways can we give honor and respect to our ancestors—the mothers and fathers of the past who were the pioneers of our faith?
2. What does it mean to honor our parents? As parents, how can we teach our children to honor us?
3. Describe or give an example of honorable parents. In

what ways do their children see God in them?

4. What does the promise "Honor your parents and your days will be long" mean to you? What implications might this have for your family? Your community? Society in general?

5. What does obedience to the seventh Commandment, "You shall not commit adultery," demonstrate? In what other ways are we to show love and loyalty to our spouses? How do these things help to build a strong family?

6. Do you agree that the home is the most basic and important unit in our society? What can we do—as individual families and as a church family—to help strengthen the family? What possible impact do you believe this might have on our society?

Chapter 12: The Power of Respect and Goodwill

1. We see in this chapter that the Commandment "You shall not murder" means that we should always hold human life as sacred. Is there ever an exception? Why, or why not? What support for your answer can you find in the Gospels?

2. How can stealing sometimes be a subtle sin? Are there times when we do not recognize our own dishonesty? Can you give examples? What can help us to be more honest in all our dealings?

3. Read Ephesians 4:25-32. How do Paul's instructions support or clarify the ninth Commandment, "You shall not bear false witness against your neighbor"? How is speaking the truth in love different from simply being truthful? What does Paul have to say about this?

151

4. In this chapter, we see that to covet is not only to desire something that someone else has, but it is also to be envious, jealous, or resentful of others. The elder son in the parable of the prodigal son demonstrates covetousness. What other characters or stories in the Bible provide an example of the sin of covetousness? What would you say is the opposite of covetousness?

Chapter 13: And Along Came Jesus

1. How is the Law of Love a new Commandment?
2. How would you define "sacrificial love"? Give an example from your own experience.
3. Do you agree that love is the real sign of discipleship? Why, or why not?
4. Read Colossians 3:1-14. What specific instructions do we find here for continuing Christ's ministry of love?